Strategic Management of Biotech Firms: Innovation, Competition and Value Creation in the Knowledge Economy

Authored by

Paola Olimpia Achard
Department of Industrial and Information Engineering & Economics, University of L'Aquila
L'Aquila, Italy

Strategic Management of Biotech Firms - Innovation Competition and Value Creation in the Knowledge Economy

Author: Paola Olimpia Achard

ISBN (Online): 979-8-89881-594-3

ISBN (Print): 979-8-89881-595-0

ISBN (Paperback): 979-8-89881-596-7

Published by Bentham Science Publishers Pte. Ltd. Singapore,

First published in 2026.

Bentham Science Publishers Pte. Ltd.
No. 9 Raffles Place
Office No. 26-01
Singapore 048619
Singapore
Email: subscriptions@benthamscience.net

BENTHAM SCIENCE

CONTENTS

FOREWORD i

PREFACE iii

DEDICATION iv

ACKNOWLEDGEMENTS v

CHAPTER 1 THE BIOTECH SECTOR: ANALYSIS OF THE EXTERNAL ENVIRONMENTAL FACTORS 1
- INTRODUCTION 1
- THE RELEVANT EXTERNAL CONTEXT: ANALYSIS OF THE MACRO-ENVIRONMENT 5
- RELEVANT FACTORS IN THE EUROPEAN BIOTECH MACRO-ENVIRONMENT 6
  - Political 6
  - Government 8
  - Economic 9
  - Social 10
  - Technological 11
  - Environmental 11
  - Legal 12
- SECTOR ANALYSIS: CHARACTERISTICS AND CRITICAL SUCCESS FACTORS 12
  - Key Data of the Biotech Sector in Europe 13
  - Key Data of the Biotech Sector in Italy 15
  - Competitiveness and Critical Success Factors of Biotech Firms 18
  - Analysis of Horizontal Competitive Forces 19
  - Analysis of Vertical Competitive Forces 21
- EVIDENCE AND CURRENT DEVELOPMENTS IN THE SECTOR 23
  - Focus on Spain 23
  - Focus on the UK 25
- CONCLUDING REMARKS 27

CHAPTER 2 MANAGING COMPETITION THROUGH STRATEGIC COLLABORATIONS 29
- INTRODUCTION 29
- INTERORGANIZATIONAL COLLABORATIONS: RELEVANT STRATEGIC ELEMENTS 30
  - Objectives 32
  - Supporting factors and barriers 33
  - Governance 34
  - Possible Forms and Types of IORs 35
- CROSS-SECTOR COLLABORATIONS AS A WAY OF VALUE CREATION 38
  - Advantages and Strategic Motivations for Cross-Sector Collaborations 40
  - Challenges and Managerial Implications 42
- STRATEGIC EVOLUTION OF COLLABORATIONS: MERGERS & ACQUISITIONS 43
  - Mergers & Acquisitions as Exit Strategies 44
- CONCLUDING REMARKS 50

CHAPTER 3 MANAGING INNOVATION: BUSINESS MODELS AND STRATEGIC CONFIGURATIONS IN BIOTECH FIRMS 52
- INTRODUCTION 52
- BUSINESS MODELS FOR INNOVATION MANAGEMENT 53
  - The Architecture of the Business Model in Biotech Firms 54

FOCUS ON RESEARCH 55
Valorization of Intellectual Property 55
Value System and Network: Partnerships and Collaborative Relationships 56
Cost Structure and Revenue Streams 56
Centrality of Risk Management 56
Typical Configurations and Evolutionary Perspectives of Business Models 57
The Role of Policy and Scientific Clusters 59
Focus on Business Models in Italy 59
Focus on Business Models in Spain 60
Focus on Business Models in the UK 60
Focus on Business Models in South Korea 61
Key Challenges and Future Perspectives 61
Balancing Specialization with Diversification 61
Prolonged Development Timelines and Regulatory Uncertainty 61
Global Competition and the Need for International Expansion 62
Artificial Intelligence and Ecosystem-Based Innovation in the Strategic Transformation of Biotech Firms 62
CONCLUDING REMARKS 69

CHAPTER 4 VALUE-GENERATING ACTIVITIES AND STRATEGIC RESOURCES IN BIOTECH FIRMS 70
INTRODUCTION 70
MANAGEMENT OF VALUE-GENERATING ACTIVITIES 71
Infrastructure Activities 72
Human Resource Management 73
Technology Development 73
Procurement 73
Inbound Logistics 74
Operations (Production and Core Activities) 74
Outbound Logistics 75
Marketing and Sales 75
Services 75
Interdependence of Primary and Supporting Activities 76
RESOURCES AND COMPETENCIES 76
CONCLUDING REMARKS 78

CHAPTER 5 STRATEGIC MARKETING, INTELLECTUAL PROPERTY, AND SUSTAINABLE VALUE CREATION 80
INTRODUCTION 80
STRATEGIC MARKETING FOR INNOVATION: CREATION, MANAGEMENT, AND VALORIZATION OF INTELLECTUAL PROPERTY 81
THE CONTRIBUTION OF BIOTECH FIRMS TO SUSTAINABLE DEVELOPMENT 84
CONCLUDING REMARKS 86

GENERAL CONCLUSION 88

REFERENCES 91
REFERENCES 91

SUBJECT INDEX 108

FOREWORD

Biotechnology is commonly defined as the use of living organisms or their components to produce substances beneficial to humankind. In this regard, it is noteworthy that even in prehistory, beverages and foods resulting from fermentation and leavening processes - such as wine, beer, and bread - were already being produced. At that time, however, the mechanisms facilitating the transformation of natural inputs into everyday food products remained unknown. It was only through Louis Pasteur's research that humanity gained an understanding of the microorganisms responsible for these transformations; consequently, Pasteur is frequently cited as the "father" of biotechnology. This was followed, in the early 1970s, by the development of recombinant DNA technology by Cohen and Boyer, which enables the isolation and excision of short DNA sequences and their subsequent transfer into the genomes of other cells, thereby modifying one or more genes. This milestone marked the birth of the innovative or advanced biotechnology sector, of which Genentech -founded in 1977 by Boyer himself - represents the progenitor. Since then, there has been an ongoing expansion in the number of firms basing their business models on these technologies. Depending on the source consulted, the modern biotechnology market is valued between $1.7 and $2.5 trillion, with projections suggesting it could reach nearly $4 trillion by 2030. This magnitude is undoubtedly significant, explaining the keen interest of the financial world and policymakers in a sector that has become strategic for many nations. From a business management perspective, however, the most compelling element lies in the unique characteristics of this industry. It is composed of a growing number of firms applying these technologies across diverse fields, ranging from pharmaceuticals and agriculture to industrial applications, the environment, and marine biology. These entrepreneurial entities operate within a highly innovative context characterized by a profound structural complexity that links diverse actors, including established and startup firms, universities, and both public and private research centers. These factors render the management of biotech firms a subject of particular interest to management scholars, offering numerous avenues for investigating the managerial methods and tools they employ. In this light, the contribution provided by my colleague and friend, Paola O. Achard - based on her teaching and research experience - constitutes an important resource. It serves both students of management courses - including those increasingly prevalent within life sciences curricula - and managers tasked with developing innovative approaches where elements such as innovation, competition, and cooperation must achieve a harmonious balance. Among the primary strengths of this book is its focus on the coexistence and interaction of these three elements, complemented by a thorough characterization of the reference context. In this field, technological, economic, social, and regulatory aspects intersect continuously, to a degree far greater than in other sectors, including those with high technological intensity. Simultaneously, the text is characterized by a seamless integration of a rigorous scientific approach - grounded in management theory - with the analysis of specific empirical cases, which facilitates a deeper understanding of the specificities of such a complex sector.

Regarding the latter, the decision to offer a comparative perspective spanning Europe (with a focus on the United Kingdom, Spain, and Italy) and Asia (South Korea) is particularly commendable, as it allows for a comparison of business models adopted in economically, socially, and institutionally distinct contexts. In my role as University Delegate for Technology Transfer, Third-Party Research, and Spin-off Creation at the University of L'Aquila, I particularly appreciated the part of the volume devoted to the strategic management of innovation processes. These processes are notably complex and risky in this sector, due to the long timelines and substantial financial resources required. Within these processes, a fundamental role is played by the collaboration between universities and industry

- a relationship that is not always straightforward but which, if managed effectively, can become a win-win scenario for both parties, as well as for the broader economic and social system.

Luciano Fratocchi
Management Engineering
Department of Industrial and Information
Engineering & Economics
University of L'Aquila
L'Aquila, Italy

Preface

This volume is conceived as a strategic management textbook on biotechnology firms, designed to provide students and interested readers with a clear, structured, and research-informed analytical framework. Biotech firms represent a particularly relevant context for analyzing competition in the knowledge economy, as they operate under conditions of high scientific and technological uncertainty, stringent regulatory environments, significant capital requirements, and complex inter-organizational networks involving universities, research centers, investors, pharmaceutical companies, and public institutions. The book adopts a didactic approach, interpreting managerial phenomena through established management theories, integrated with empirical evidence and the sector-specific characteristics of a knowledge-intensive industry. Each chapter, therefore, combines theoretical concepts, managerial implications, and a critical analysis of key industry trends, supporting both the acquisition of foundational knowledge and the development of analytical skills applicable to case studies, assignments, and projects. The volume is structured into five chapters organized around three analytical blocks. The first block addresses the competitive context of biotech firms, focusing on macro-environmental factors and industry structure, including critical success factors and competitive forces. The second block examines interorganizational collaborations as strategic levers, analysing alliances, cross-sector partnerships, and mergers and acquisitions as mechanisms for knowledge access, risk sharing, and strategic evolution. The third block focuses on the governance of innovation processes within biotech firms. In this perspective, the analysis examines business models, value-generating activities, strategic resources, intellectual property management, and sustainable value-creation dynamics. The book is primarily intended for undergraduate and postgraduate students in economics and management, but it may also be used in postgraduate and executive education contexts. It further offers an analytical framework for researchers, managers, and policymakers interested in understanding strategic choices and innovation trajectories in biotechnology firms, systematically linking theory, research evidence, and managerial implications.

Paola Olimpia Achard
Department of Industrial and Information
Engineering & Economics, University of L'Aquila
L'Aquila, Italy

DEDICATION

To M., for the support along the way.

And to A., who remains with me.

ACKNOWLEDGEMENTS

The preparation of this volume results from a long-standing scholarly and teaching trajectory, developed through continuous interaction with colleagues, students, and academic institutions. The author gratefully acknowledges colleagues who, through scientific dialogue and academic collaboration, contributed to consolidating the analytical framework and managerial perspectives developed throughout the book. Special recognition is extended to the students at the University of L'Aquila enrolled in undergraduate and postgraduate programmes in economics, management, and biotechnology, whose critical engagement in the classroom contributed to shaping the empirical grounding and conceptual framing of the models, decision-making logics, and strategic interpretations presented in this volume. Chapter 2 benefited from the scholarly contribution of Chiara Bellini, who participated in the development of its conceptual architecture, contributed to content refinement, and supported the preparation of visual materials. Responsibility for the final content and interpretations remains solely with the author. The author also acknowledges Leonardo Ioannucci for his assistance with bibliographic research and documentary analysis, which support the empirical and contextual sections of the book. Finally, the author acknowledges the academic institutions and national and international research environments that provided opportunities for structured discussion and intellectual exchange, contributing to the refinement of the strategic and organizational analyses presented herein.

Paola O. Achard
Department of Industrial and Information
Engineering & Economics, University of L'Aquila
L'Aquila, Italy

CHAPTER 1

The Biotech Sector: Analysis of the External Environmental Factors

Abstract: This chapter provides a systematic analysis of the external conditions shaping the strategic choices of biotechnology firms operating in Europe. The analysis is articulated across two complementary levels: the macro-environment and the competitive environment. At the macro level, three interdependent factors are examined *i.e.*, political-institutional orientation, technological trajectories, and regulatory frameworks, which together create both constraints and opportunities for biotechnology firms, particularly in the red biotechnology subsector. The chapter highlights how research and development investments, digitalization processes, and European policy initiatives influence access to financial resources, stimulate cross-sector collaborations among healthcare, pharmaceutical, and ICT actors, and encourage the development of innovation clusters and networks. At the sectoral level, the European biotech sector is characterized by high barriers to entry, low substitutability, strong supplier specialization, and medium-to-high customer bargaining power. Consequently, critical success factors include firms' ability to absorb and integrate knowledge, manage strategic partnerships along the innovation chain, and translate scientific research into scalable therapeutic and industrial solutions. The chapter concludes by outlining managerial and policy implications for strengthening European competitiveness in knowledge-intensive industries.

Keywords: Biotech sector, Competitive forces, Critical success factors, External environment, Innovation ecosystems, Knowledge-based firms, PESTEL.

INTRODUCTION

For more than two decades, new applications in healthcare, agriculture and food production, and environmental protection, alongside scientific breakthroughs, have brought about profound changes in the knowledge base underpinning the life sciences and biotechnologies. Significant investments in Research and Development (R&D) are driving the growth of the biotech sector at global scale. These investments are shaped by demographic changes, increased life expectancy, transformations in biomedical models, social globalization, and the substantial expansion of access to healthcare services. In fact, innovations in the biotech sector are disruptive and have a direct impact on social and economic well-being,

Paola Olimpia Achard

as well as on planetary sustainability. The growing focus on sustainable development (United Nations, 2025) is presenting new challenges for biotech firms. Firms operating within the sector can make a significant contribution by creating solutions that are in harmony with, and conducive to, the long-term balance of living systems (European Biotechnology Network, 2025). These developments have also been affected by the changes brought about by the COVID-19 pandemic (Tabish, 2020). The pandemic underscored the strategic importance of the biotech sector for global health and security, highlighting the critical role of biotech firms in preventing, treating, and managing the effects of pandemics.

All the aspects referenced thus far highlight the strategic significance the biotech sector has assumed globally over the past decade, prompting scholars in the managerial field to examine the strategic profiles of modern biotech firms. The study of the strategic configuration of biotech firms, in turn, opens the way to important analyses and reflections on the modes of value creation (Porter & Kramer, 2019) that firms activate through their activities, processes, and involved actors.

The biotech sector is knowledge-intensive, with value creation predominantly oriented towards generating new knowledge, which is subsequently leveraged, disseminated, and translated into novel products and/or services. Knowledge represents a competitive asset (Mowery, Oxley & Silverman, 1996). Indeed, competition on a global scale is fundamentally grounded in the creation, acquisition, absorption, sharing, and transfer of new knowledge (Doz, 2023). The generation of new knowledge significantly affects both the quality and quantity of innovation-related products and processes. Concurrently, the capacity to integrate knowledge has profound implications for innovation performance, that is, the extent to which a firm is capable not only of generating innovative ideas but, more critically, of converting them into tangible and sustainable outcomes over time (Mardani *et al.*, 2018). Biotech firms strategically harness innovation to secure competitive advantage (Porter, 1985), at both local and global levels, and to adapt their strategic orientations in response to the evolving demands of the external environment.

Recent data show that the health sector accounts for more than one-fifth of the global R&D investments (European Commission, 2025a). This phenomenon is attributable to the increasing presence of biotech and pharmaceutical firms among the principal corporate investors in R&D over the past ten years. As of 2024, the global biotech sector generated approximately 559 billion US dollars in revenue, comprising 12,487 firms, reflecting a 4.6% growth from 2023 (IBISWorld, 2025).

In Europe, as of 2022 (Statista, 2024a), the latest year for which data are available, slightly more than 6,500 biotech firms are operating, as depicted in Fig. (**1**).

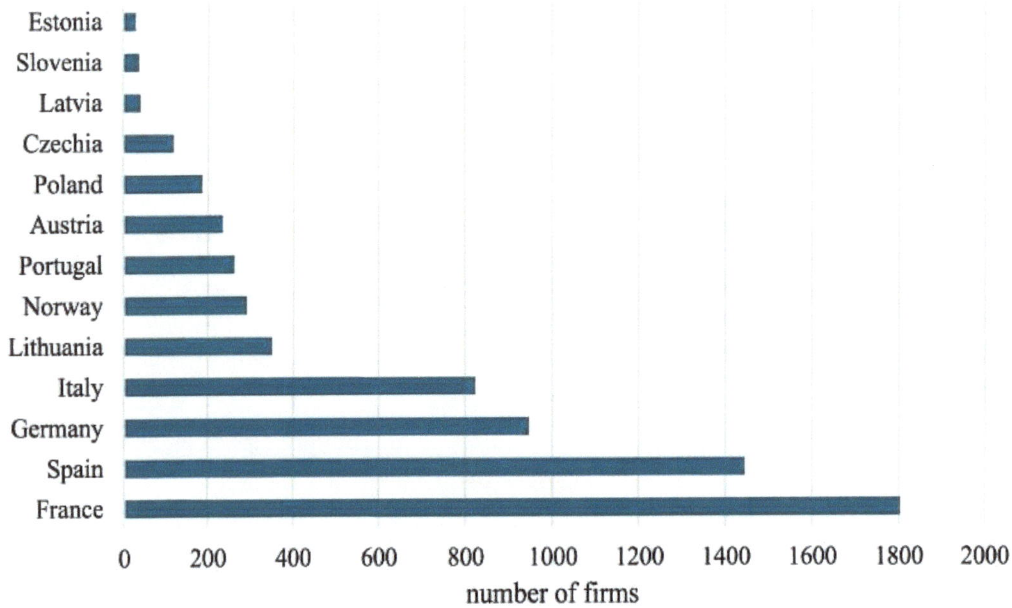

Fig. (1). Distribution of biotech firms in Europe (Statista, 2024b).

A biotech firm is defined as a firm engaged in key biotechnological activities, such as the application of at least one biotechnological technique to produce goods or services and/or the execution of biotechnological R&D activities (OECD, 2005). The differentiated and heterogeneous nature of biotech firms does not permit a clear-cut classification. In this volume, the color-coding criterion (DaSilva, 2004) is employed, allowing the distinction of biotech firms by their predominant subsector of activity. The most widely recognized colors are three. Fig. (**2**) illustrates the distribution of firms by subsector affiliation in Italy: red (medical-pharmacological area), green (agri-food area), and white (Gene-based Bioindustries).

Firms specializing in genomics, proteomics, and enabling technologies (Key Enabling Technologies, KETs, or General Purpose Technologies, GPTs) play a transversal role across all other subsectors. In addition to these three, there are five other subsectors identified in Table **1**, although an additional color (orange) is often used to designate firms involved in the dissemination of knowledge, applications, and discoveries within the biotech sector. Furthermore, it is possible to distinguish biotech firms according to their core business (Abell, 1980;

Osterwalder & Pigneur, 2010). Indeed, the Organization for Economic Co-operation and Development (OECD) identifies two broad categories of firms: (i) dedicated biotech firms (DBFs), defined as firms operating in the biotech sector whose primary activity consists of applying biotechnological techniques for the production of goods or services and/or the execution of biotechnological R&D activities; and (ii) Innovative Biotech Firms (IBFs), defined as firms operating in the biotech sector that apply biotechnological techniques with the purpose of developing new or significantly improved products or processes.

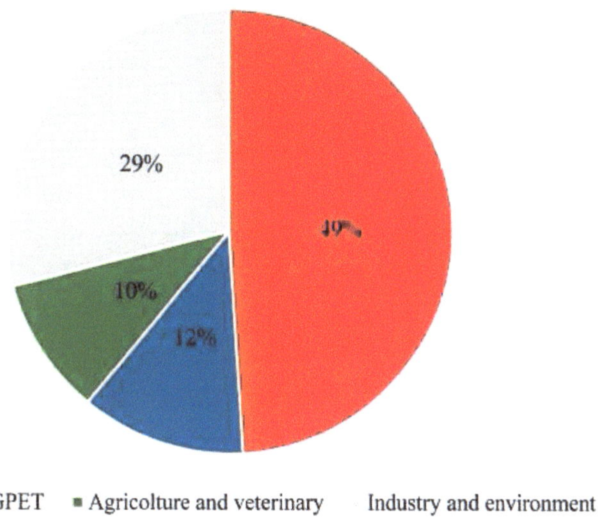

Fig. (2). Distribution of Italian biotech firms in the main subsectors (Assobiotec – Federchimica, 2023).

This chapter considers both DBFs and IBFs, with particular attention to those operating in the red subsector dedicated to the health area. Specifically, the objective is to identify the macro-environmental and sectoral dynamics that shape and influence the strategic decisions of biotech firms operating in Europe. The analysis of the external environment of firms is functional to the decision-making processes involved in corporate strategic planning and characterizes it (Mintzberg, 1983; 1994).

Table 1. The color classifications of the biotech sector (own elaboration, based on DaSilva, 2004, Kafarski, 2012).

Color	Area of Activity
Red	Health, medicine, and diagnostics
Yellow	Food biotechnology and nutritional sciences
Blu	Aquaculture, coastal and marine biotechnology

(Table 1) cont.....

Color	Area of Activity
Green	Agricultural and environmental biotechnology
Brown	Biotechnology of arid and desert regions
Black	Bioterrorism, biological warfare
Violet	Patents, publications, inventions, and intellectual property rights
White	Gene-based bioindustries
Gold	Bioinformatics and nanobiotechnology
Grey	Classical fermentation and bioprocessing technologies

THE RELEVANT EXTERNAL CONTEXT: ANALYSIS OF THE MACRO-ENVIRONMENT

Several factors demonstrate that the European biotech sector is characterized by strong competitive dynamism. Therefore, to outline effective strategies, it is essential for firms to adequately understand the characteristics of the relevant context in which they operate (Bourgeois III, 1980). The relevant context, in turn, is articulated into two distinct levels of environment, which are the broader context (or macro-environment) and the competitive environment (or sector). Specifically, this paragraph delves into the analysis of the macro-environment that characterizes biotech firms in Europe.

The broader context comprises the set of actors and conditions that represent significant constraints and opportunities for firms, and which, consequently, influence their strategic decisions (Caroli, 2021). To determine which macro-environmental factors exert varying degrees of influence on European biotech firms and consequently shape their strategic choices and behaviors, the PEST analysis is applied (Yüksel, 2012). In relation to the sector under examination, it is appropriate to classify the external environment factors into six main categories, from which the acronym PESTEL is derived: political, economic, social, technological, environmental, and legal. Without a clear understanding of the key features of the European biotech macro-environment, firms are unable to make appropriate decisions (Çitilci & Akbalik, 2020). In environments marked by a high degree of competitive dynamism, it is appropriate, from the firm's perspective, to consider and manage the interconnections existing between corporate strategy and organizational structure, environment and organizational structure, strategy formulation (Mintzberg, 2017), and environment (Miller & Friesen, 1983).

PESTEL analysis constitutes a tool that can be activated as a process (Fig. **3**), aimed at identifying only those factors that are both relevant and mutually interrelated (Johnson, Whittington & Scholes, 2014; Molloy & Johnson, 2016), to avoid taking into consideration a multitude of factors that are not actually significant. The relevant factors are those most capable of influencing the strategic behavior of firms operating within the sector under investigation, as well as those in related and/or complementary sectors (for example, the healthcare sector).

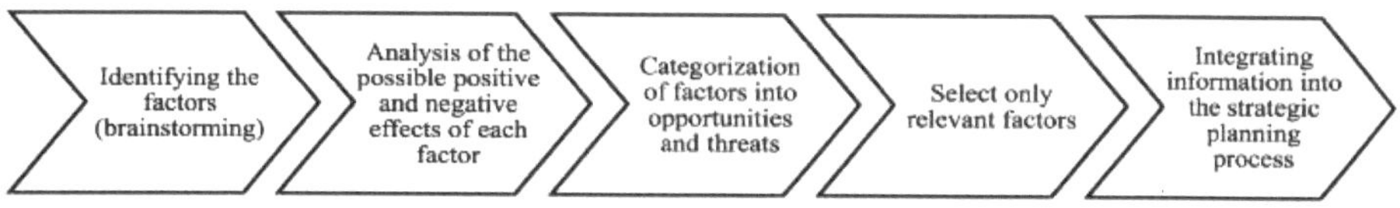

Fig. (3). Macroenvironment Analysis Process (PESTEL) (own elaboration).

It is important to emphasize that the analysis of the macro-environment does not represent a fixed and definitive framework (Ho, 2014), but rather a framework composed of interdependent factors that requires periodic monitoring by firms operating in the sector. The following paragraph provides an in-depth examination of the most representative factors of the European biotech macro-environment.

RELEVANT FACTORS IN THE EUROPEAN BIOTECH MACRO-ENVIRONMENT

Each macro-environmental factor can be articulated into two interdependent sets: actors and conditions. Actors consist of firms and/or organizations that pursue specific objectives. Conditions, on the other hand, are partly structural and partly the direct or indirect outcomes of actors' behaviors or, more broadly, of other factors in the environment (Fontana & Caroli, 2013). A detailed analysis of the relevant factors in the European biotech macro-environment is reported in the following sections.

Political

For over two decades, with the aim of actively contributing to the growth of the biotech sector, the European Commission has outlined Life Sciences Biotechnology – A Strategy for Europe. This European strategy has clearly highlighted how life sciences and biotechnology are widely considered among the most promising frontier technologies of the coming decades. Life sciences and biotechnology have been defined as enabling technologies because, similarly to information technology, they can be applied to a wide range of purposes. Based on the scientific discoveries achieved, the explosion of knowledge concerning living systems is destined to produce a continuous flow of new applications (European Commission, 2025b). In 2018, the role of biotechnology was further reinforced through the adoption of the Bioeconomy Strategy. This orientation aimed to position the bioeconomy among the European Commission's political and institutional priorities and, consequently, those of the Member States.

In 2019, an additional relevant programming act, from a strategic perspective, was approved, namely the European Green Deal. The European Green Deal is a set of strategic initiatives designed to accompany Europe through a process of green transition, with the ultimate objective of achieving climate neutrality by 2050 (European Commission, 2002). The Green Deal is a programming framework that serves as a stimulus to initiate a series of other proposals and projects across various mutually interdependent fields (European Commission, 2019). For illustrative purposes, reference can be made to strategies concerning biodiversity, climate, and food. In all the mentioned aspects, biotechnology plays a key role. More recently, the strategic document of the European Association for Bioindustries (EuropaBio) identified eight fundamental pillars outlining how firms operating in the life sciences sectors will contribute to realizing a healthier, more sustainable Europe. These pillars are capital financing, skills, R&D and innovation, Intellectual Property (IP), production systems, digitization, regional development, and global competitiveness (EuropaBio, 2021).

More recently, the Eu4Health Program 2021-2027 (European Commission, 2020a), a strategic plan adopted to confront the COVID-19 crisis and to prepare Europe to effectively respond to future pandemic emergencies, has been adopted. The plan clearly underscores that matters pertaining to public health are of utmost priority. Consequently, it has identified a comprehensive set of areas to intervene in to strengthen their effectiveness. Among these, particular attention is given to the Pharmaceutical Strategy for Europe, which aims to delineate a renewed regulatory framework for the pharmaceutical sector, with a stronger orientation towards promoting research and innovation.

The other two programs are also worth mentioning: the Digital Europe Program and the Horizon Europe 2021-2027 framework program. The Digital Europe Program (European Commission, 2020b), designed to stimulate the digital transition, is a transversal programming act across all other initiatives and aims to increase Europe's competitiveness through intervention in five key areas, *i.e.*, supercomputing, Artificial Intelligence (AI), cybersecurity, advanced digital skills, and widespread use of digital technologies within the economy and society. Horizon Europe 2021-2027 (European Commission, 2020c) is the European Union's framework program for research and innovation, aimed at reinforcing Europe's competitive positioning through the strengthening of scientific and technological areas.

Within the scope of political factors, it is appropriate to highlight the presence of certain actors whose actions are determinative for firms operating in the biotech sector. First, it should be noted that the European Medicines Agency (EMA) promotes scientific excellence in the evaluation and supervision of medicinal products for the benefit of human and animal health within the European Union. The European Federation of Pharmaceutical Industries and Associations (EFPIA) represents the entire European biopharmaceutical sector. EFPIA's strategic aim is to promote a collaborative environment that enables firms to innovate, discover, develop, and deliver new therapies and vaccines for people in Europe. The European Patients' Forum (EPF), on the other hand, is an independent, non-governmental, non-profit organization that brings together patient organizations from across Europe. EPF's objective is to protect patients who participate in the R&D processes of new products or services. Finally, it should be recalled that EuropaBio, the largest and most influential group of biotech firms in Europe, whose purpose is to engage with the European Parliament and the European Commission to influence political and institutional decision-making concerning the sector, and ERA CoBioTech, an ERANET initiative aimed at leveraging the existing synergies among the current funding mechanisms for biotechnology research in Europe.

Government

Since the early 2000s, scholars at the international level have been questioning the role of governmental institutions and science policies in promoting funding and innovating evaluation processes to support collaborative and transdisciplinary projects (McMillan, Hamilton III & Deeds 2000). Public interventions serve as catalysts that can either stimulate or hinder the emergence of biotech firms. A favorable environment for risk-taking, private financing, and technology transfer has granted the USA a competitive advantage in the sector, whereas in certain European countries, such as Germany, more centralized policies and greater regulatory caution have led to more gradual growth (Giesecke, 2000). More recent analysis demonstrates that government subsidies have a positive impact on innovation, both by increasing R&D activities and by directly promoting the introduction of innovative products and services. Within the European biotech macro-environment, there exist critical issues compared to the other two major players, the USA and China, which are connected to several factors, including long lab-to-market times, regulatory complexity, fragmentation of the capital market leading to difficulties in accessing financing, the need for multidisciplinary skill profiles, and the guarantee of economic and technological security. To support individual countries, the European Commission has intervened on multiple fronts, including regulatory simplification, incentives for R&D, financing mechanisms and skills development, intersectoral and international cooperation, and finally the promotion of demand for bio-based products and services (European Commission, 2025a). These efforts have been further supplemented by the findings of the review of the EU Bioeconomy Strategy, aimed at strengthening the industrial dimension of the biotech sector (European Commission, 2025b).

Economic

European R&D expenditure increased between 2000 and 2021. In 2021, approximately 2.15% of GDP was spent on R&D in the biotech sector. The European GDP in 2021 amounted to 14.5 trillion euros (Eurostat, 2023). Fig. (**4**) shows the annual public expenditure on R&D in the biotech sector in several European countries.

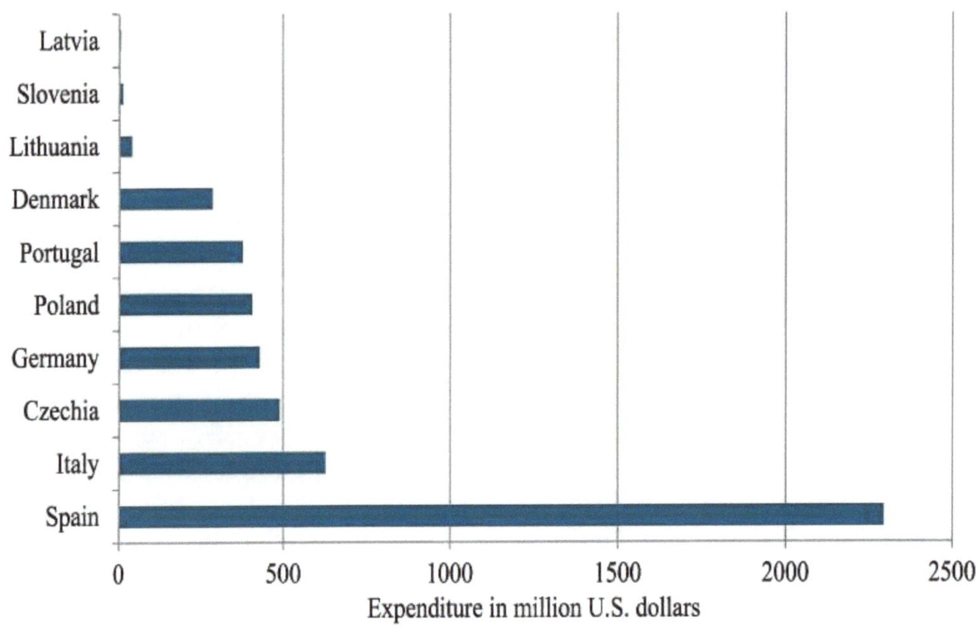

Fig. (4). Annual public spending invested in biotechnology R&D (Statista, 2025a).

Global investments in R&D in 2022 increased by 7.8%, driven primarily by European firms, which accounted for 5.9% of the increase. Four sectors were identified as the main contributors to this growth in Europe: ICT hardware, ICT software, healthcare (understood in a broad sense to also include biotech and pharmaceutical firms), and the automotive sector. Moreover, an analysis of data from the EU R&D Scoreboard 2024 indicates that, in Europe, private investments in R&D within the healthcare sector account for 20.5% of total R&D investment. In 2022, which is the most recent year for which data are available, European healthcare expenditure accounted for 10.4% of Gross Domestic Product (GDP), amounting to over 1,648 billion euros (OECD & European Commission, 2024). As of 2023, 60% of this expenditure is allocated to care and rehabilitation services, 15% to long-term healthcare provision, and 9% (equivalent to 148.32 billion euros) to preventive services, representing an increase of 3.1% compared to 2021.

Beyond expenditure data, it is essential for biotech firms to be informed about the financing sources available to support R&D. Among these, certain funds linked to strategic programs, previously highlighted within the political factors, could be mentioned. Horizon Europe 2021-2027 (€95.5 billion); Eu4Health 2021-2027 (€5.3 billion); the Digital Europe Program (€7.5 billion). Conversely, the Green Deal has established a different mechanism, binding 30% of the European Union's Multiannual Financial Framework (2021-2028) to green investments.

Social

In 2023, life expectancy at birth in Europe (OECD & European Commission, 2024) rose to 81.5 years, surpassing pre-COVID-19 pandemic levels by 0.2 years. The principal causes of death in Europe are closely linked to sustained exposure to major risk factors, including tobacco smoking, alcohol consumption, obesity, and excessive physical inactivity. Every year, over 6 million individuals across Europe suffer from cardiovascular diseases, and approximately 1.7 million people die because of circulatory system disorders. Cancer constitutes the second leading cause of mortality, following cardiovascular diseases, and in 2022, a new cancer case was diagnosed every 12 seconds. If current mortality rates and cancer incidence remain unchanged over the coming years, the number of cancer diagnoses in Europe is expected to increase by 18% by 2040 compared to 2022. Compounding this public health burden is the fact that 10% of all premature human deaths are attributable to environmental pollution.

In terms of unmet needs, new gaps have been identified in the aftermath of the pandemic emergency, due to the growing demand, particularly for medical care, primarily at the primary care level. Unmet needs for medical consultations increased from 1.7% in 2019 to 2.4% in 2023. Lastly, disparities in access to healthcare services reflect broader health inequalities, which are closely associated with underlying social factors such as educational attainment and income levels.

Technological

The biotech macro-environment is characterized by the presence of numerous product and process innovations, which, according to a forward-looking analysis, are expected to drive substantial growth in the sector over the coming years (Global Market Insights, 2021). In Europe, approximately 1,783 biotechnology patents were registered in 2023, a 23% increase since 2005 (Statista, 2025b).

Process innovations are characterized by a high degree of interdependence with the technology, healthcare, and pharmaceutical sectors. For example, R&D activities have fostered the emergence of innovative medical technologies such as 3D bioprinting and biosensors, which are employed in personal health monitoring.

Another process innovation exhibiting significant interdependencies with the healthcare sector is personalized medicine. Personalized medicine is founded on the principle that everyone's genome, interacting with environmental factors, imparts unique characteristics to complex diseases, enabling more precise diagnosis and treatment. The applications of personalized medicine will assist in treating certain hereditary genetic disorders and support the design of healthcare solutions tailored to the specific needs of individual patients. Furthermore, emerging concepts such as cell therapy, used in the treatment of oncological diseases, have the potential to provide regenerative medicine capable of inducing disease remission.

Regarding product innovations, the biopharmaceutical sector is projected to grow at a global rate of 9.2% by 2027. The increasing adoption of novel basic research methodologies, such as the use of bio-recombinant proteins, will promote the development of innovative therapeutic solutions, for example, in the treatment of numerous chronic diseases.

Environmental

The European Union contributes more to environmental degradation than many other regions worldwide. Current assessments by the European Environment Agency (2025) indicate that although the implementation of targeted policies has yielded benefits across various domains, substantial scope for improvement remains.

By way of illustration, the following key aspects are highlighted: (i) only 40% of the EU's surface waters have achieved good ecological status since 2015; (ii) 75% of European ecosystems are exposed to excessive levels of nitrogen; (iii) European biodiversity is threatened by air, soil, and water pollution; (iv) the land temperature in Europe increased from 2.04°C to 2.10°C between 2013 and 2022;

(v) between 2000 and 2019, severe droughts caused an annual loss of vegetation productivity of 3% in the affected areas; (vi) qualitative assessments conducted between 2013 and 2020 detected one or more pesticides exceeding their respective effect thresholds in 10-25% of all monitored sites.

The dimensions outlined above constitute significant incentives to increase investment in industrial and green biotechnology, with the objective of actively mitigating the detrimental impacts that environmental dynamics impose on both human and animal health.

Legal

Legal matters are fundamental to firms operating in the biotech sector, and the most significant reform process of the past 20 years is currently underway. This legislative revision will replace the existing regulatory instruments, namely: European Regulation No. 726/2004, European Directive 2001/83/EC, the Pediatric Medicines Regulation No. 1901/2006, and the Regulation on the management of rare diseases No. 141/2000/EC.

The European Commission has identified the imperative to modernize the sector from a regulatory standpoint to enhance Europe's capacity for innovation and competitiveness. The reform entails rationalizing and simplifying R&D, production, and distribution processes to make them more flexible, agile, and better suited to address contemporary demands. Nonetheless, the need to modernize the legislative framework does not entail any relaxation of the stringent authorization standards that govern the research, development, and production of pharmaceuticals and biopharmaceuticals in Europe.

The factors that characterize the European biotech macro-environment influence, in terms of constraints or opportunities, the strategic features of the competitive biotech environment, which will be examined in greater depth in the following section.

SECTOR ANALYSIS: CHARACTERISTICS AND CRITICAL SUCCESS FACTORS

The analysis of the European biotech macro-environment has enabled the identification of a set of significant factors that influence the strategic characteristics of the biotech sector in Europe in terms of: (i) strategic priorities in business management; (ii) relevant distinctive resources and competencies and the methods for their development; (iii) competitive positioning and competitive advantage; (iv) the potential profitability of the sector or the business area under consideration. In the following sections, some key data of the sector, both in

Europe and in Italy, are reported, and the critical success factors of biotech firms are analyzed, exploring the horizontal and vertical competitive forces.

Key Data of the Biotech Sector in Europe

According to the latest update by the OECD on key indicators (number of biotech firms; biotechnology R&D expenditure; public spending on biotechnology R&D; biotechnology patents) for the biotech sector (June 2023), the USA remains the global leader in the field, with the highest number of active biotech firms (2,840) and an R&D intensity value-added of 17%. Europe, despite the presence of some major biotech firms (including the world's largest one by market capitalization, *i.e.*, Novo Nordisk), does not have a widespread and uniform presence in the sector at the global level, due to a growth/decline dynamic which McKinsey & Company (2021) described as occurring at two speeds. Indeed, half of all biotech firms are currently based in France, Germany, and the UK, while most other European countries have struggled to establish themselves in the sector.

Despite this dual-speed growth, biotechnology has been one of the fastest-growing sectors in Europe between 2008 and 2018 (WifOr Institute, 2020). Actually, the UK continues to experience growth. It has played a pivotal role in the development of numerous innovative technologies across various pathological areas and has hosted 35% of all biotech start-ups in Europe since 2012 (BioIndustry Association, 2025).

Belgium, the Netherlands, and Switzerland are also experiencing growth, albeit at considerably lower rates. In contrast, in France, Germany, and Sweden, biotech start-up activity has slowed in recent years. The COVID-19 pandemic has only exacerbated this divide, with some firms that already held a substantial market share increasing it further, while many countries that were previously well-positioned in the sector have experienced a slight yet persistent decline.

The sector's revenue growth rate increased substantially immediately following the pandemic crisis, primarily driven by the performance of the five leading firms in Europe and the USA. Indeed, in 2021, growth exceeded 5%, whereas in 2022, in the absence of the initial pandemic impact, growth reverted to pre-crisis levels of approximately 4 percentage points (EY, 2023).

Fig. (**5**) illustrates the linear trend of the biotech sector's growth (Europe and the USA), with a clear peak corresponding to the impact of the COVID-19 pandemic.

After 2020, largely due to the COVID-19 pandemic, the market value of many firms in the sector (including in Europe) began to increase more sharply.

According to figures from the beginning of 2024, five European firms are among the top 25 biotech firms globally by market capitalization (Table **2**).

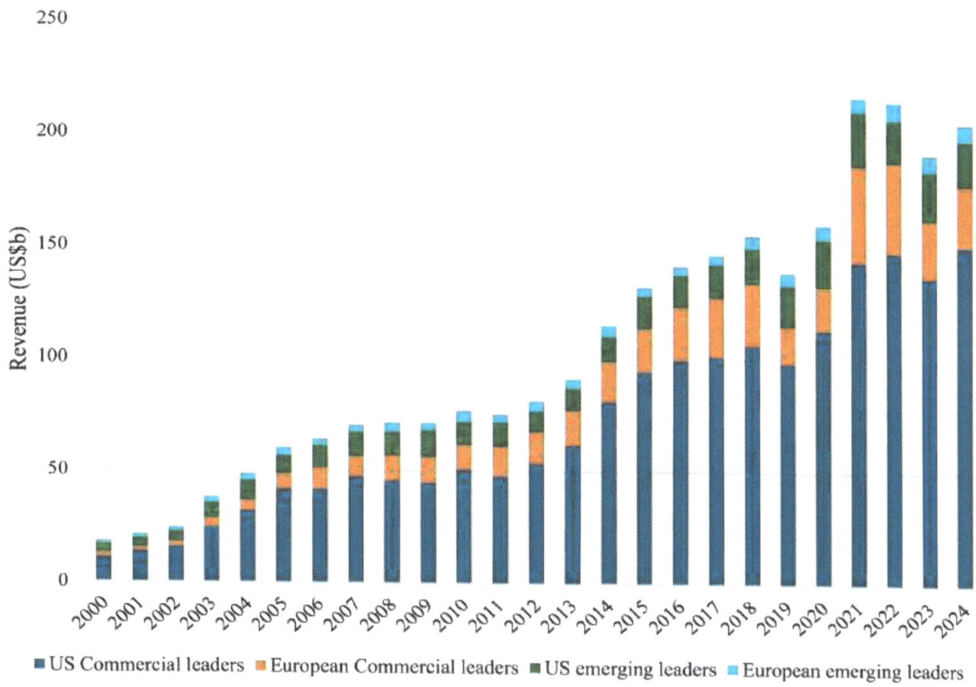

Fig. (5). Growth of the biotech sector by turnover in Europe and the USA (E&Y & Assobiotec-Federchimica, 2025).

Table 2. Largest biotech companies in the world by market capitalization (own elaboration, based on Philippidis, 2024; Labiotech, 2023a).

Name of the Company	Market Capitalization (Billion $)	Increase (2023 to 2024)	Country
Novo Nordisk	$430.96	+ 16.0%	Denmark
Thermo Fisher Scientific	$189.20	- 10.1%	USA
Amgen	$143.98	+ 14.9%	USA
Gilead Sciences	$98.41	- 1.6%	USA
Regeneron Pharmaceuticals	$91.51	+ 4.4%	USA
Vertex Pharmaceuticals	$90.24	+ 1.6%	USA
CSL	$84.82	- 16.4%	Australia
Chugai Pharmaceutical	$60.86	+ 32.7%	Japan
Daiichi Sankyo	$54.33	- 21.9%	Japan
Seagen[a]	$41.31	+ 10.2%	USA

(Table 2) cont.....

Name of the Company	Market Capitalization (Billion $)	Increase (2023 to 2024)	Country
Jiangsu Hengrui Medicine	$40.59	- 12.4%	China
Samsung Biologics	$38.31	- 13.2%	South Korea
Agilent Technologies	$37.16	- 7.3%	USA
Sunpharma	$35.54	+ 23.7%	India
Biogen	$34.68	- 22.4%	USA
WuXi AppTec	$31.46	+ 7.3%	China
Moderna	$30.61	- 39.5%	USA
Lonza	$27.77	- 37.4%	Switzerland
Argenx	$26.79	+ 22.8%	Netherlands
BioNTech	$24.79	- 21.2%	Germany
Alnylam Pharmaceuticals	$21.34	- 13.5%	USA
Genmab	$21.09	- 23.2%	Denmark
BeiGene	$19.53	- 29.0%	China
Illumina	$17.93	- 41.8%	USA
Celltrion	$17.73	-4.4%	Soth Korea
[a]Seagen has been acquired by Pfizer in December 2023 for 43 billion $			

The list in Table **2** does not include pharmaceutical firms with a longstanding tradition in the development of non-biological small molecule drugs, such as AstraZeneca, a British-Swedish biopharmaceutical firm with a market capitalization exceeding $200 billion (early 2024). Indeed, although AstraZeneca is present in the sector, its core business does not focus on biotechnology.

Key Data of the Biotech Sector in Italy

In Italy, the growth trajectory of the biotech sector is analogous to that of the European context, considering that, as shown in Table **3** and Fig. (**6**), biotech firms have increased in number and turnover in a modest yet steady manner (Assobiotec–Federchimica, 2023; International Trade Administration, 2024). It is particularly interesting to analyze, in combination, two data points in Table **3**: the trend in the number of biotechnology employees and the trend in the number of biotechnology R&D employees. While the former has begun to decline in recent years (although it had remained relatively stable even in earlier periods), the number of employees involved in R&D has continued to increase, indicating an increasing need of human resources in R&D activities.

Most of the Italian firms in the biotech sector fall within the red category (Health), while the other three most common types are: Genomics, Proteomics, and

Enabling Technologies (GPTA), Industry and Environment (grey), and Agriculture and Animal Husbandry (green). Considering turnover instead of the number of firms, it can be easily understood why the biopharmaceutical subsector receives the greatest attention and is often mistakenly regarded as representative of the entire biotech sector. In fact, red biotech firms in Italy account for 49 percent of the total number of firms, but represent as much as 74 percent of total turnover, thus constituting the clear majority within the sector (Assobiotec–Federchimica, 2023).

Table 3. Key data on biotech Italian firms (Assobiotec–Federchimica, 2023): economic values in billion Euros, employees in thousand people.

Year	2015	2016	2017	2018	2019	2020	2021	2022
Number of firms	657	730	746	759	796	787	806	823
Biotech revenue	10.1	10.7	11.1	12.1	11.0	11.1	13.5	13.6
R&D investments	1.56	1.55	1.61	1.63	1.73	1.76	1.81	1.84
R&D biotech investments	0.46	0.47	0.51	0.54	0.55	0.59	0.56	0,58
Biotech employees	12.4	13.3	13.7	14.0	14.1	14.4	13.8	13.7
Biotech R&D employees	3.96	4.07	4.43	4.61	4.72	4.88	4.87	4.94

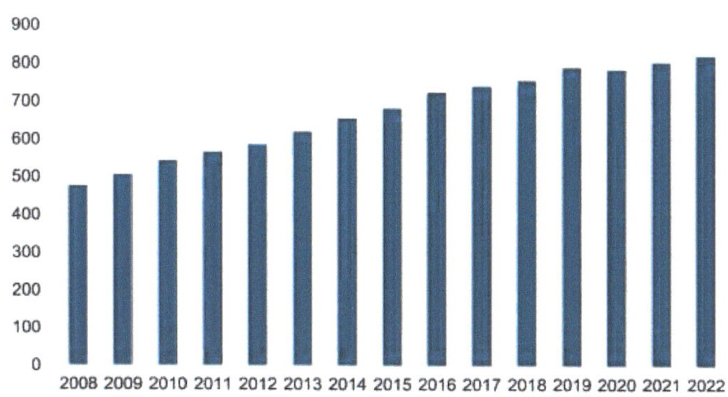

Fig. (6). Growth of the biotech sector in Italy (by number of firms) (Assobiotec–Federchimica, 2023).

Fig. (7) illustrates the sector's composition based on firm size, which closely resembles the overall distribution of businesses across various sectors in Italy. The vast majority are micro-firms (with fewer than 10 employees) and small firms (with fewer than 50 employees). Historically, these types of firms have been the most vulnerable due to their limited diversification and smaller capital reserves. However, in recent years, this trend has reversed, resulting in increased financial solvency and, consequently, reduced fragility. Fragile firms are generally defined as those no longer capable of operating under normal market conditions or covering their debt costs with current profits, thereby becoming dependent on creditors to continue their existence. Despite overall improvements in the solvency of small businesses, the biochemical and pharmaceutical sector remains fragile, according to the 2022 Cerved report on Small and Medium Firms (SMEs) (Cerved, 2022).

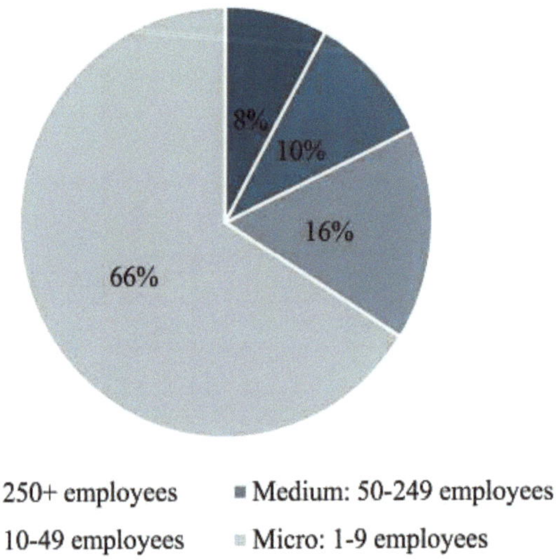

Fig. (7). Distribution of Italian biotech firms (Assobiotec–Federchimica, 2023).

Regarding the geographical distribution of biotech firms, Italy's situation closely reflects the broader economic context, with higher concentration in the northern regions (Fig. **8**).

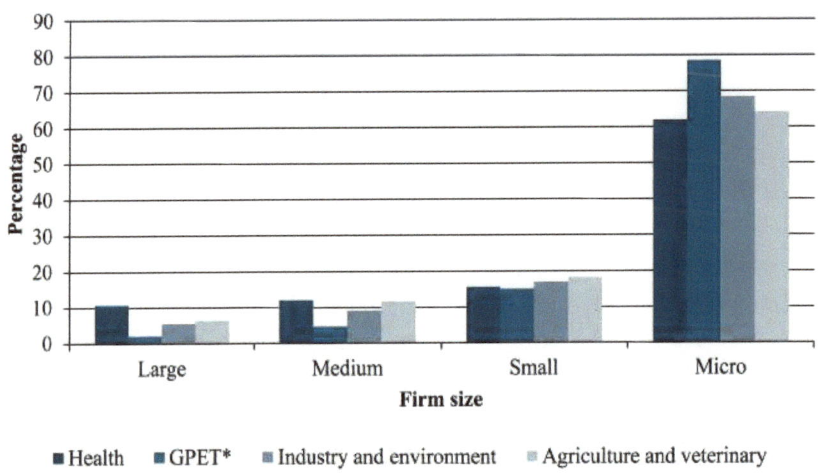

Fig. (8). Distribution of Italian biotech firms by subsector and size (Assobiotec–Federchimica, 2023).

Although some differences emerge when examining sector turnover rather than the number of firms, the concentration remains pronounced in the northern regions and, indeed, is even more marked. Moreover, certain central and southern regions, such as Lazio and Puglia, have a comparatively higher concentration of biotechnology turnover, which can be attributed, at least partly, to the presence of a limited number of large biotech firms within these territories.

Competitiveness and Critical Success Factors of Biotech Firms

The competitiveness of a sector comprises two distinct elements: competitive forces and critical success factors. The former represent pressures, either negative or positive, to which firms are subjected, while the latter are the strategic choices that allow firms to obtain a competitive advantage over their rivals (Porter, 1989; 2008). Indeed, within a sector, there are relevant factors, often summarized under the term 'competitive context', that act as forces that either hinder or facilitate the achievement of the strategic objectives of firms operating in the same sector. At the same time, there are variables on which firms can intervene through strategic decisions, significantly influencing their competitive position within the sector. These variables are defined as critical success factors and constitute the key to business success, more formally known as competitive advantage (Fontana & Caroli, 2013; Hofer & Schendel, 1978; Lin & Lekhawipat, 2023).

Starting with the example of the biopharmaceutical subsector, it is evolving at an increasingly rapid pace in Europe and globally, driven by innovations in the technologies underpinning drug development and the creation of niche markets that facilitate the entry of new actors (Porumboiu, 2020). The nature of drug discovery and development is beginning to transform due to the application of data science techniques such as AI, the availability of extensive chemical and pharmacological databases, and advancements in computational sciences and bioengineering, and the application of engineering principles to the design of biological drugs (Moradi & Dass, 2022). These technologies offer the potential to accelerate the development of targeted drugs and products, for example, by enabling rapid data screening to identify potential candidates or by facilitating more cost-effective pharmacological trials. Consequently, they constitute the critical success factors of this subsector (Hofer *et al.*, 2022).

Other critical factors for the biotech sector are the following (IQS, 2023): (i) knowledge and the capacity for its transfer, which, through the development of technological clusters, lead firms toward innovation and, consequently, transformation; (ii) the integration of naturalness into products intended for a generalized market, understood as a convergence with the increasing demand for natural products, and not to be mistaken for a substitution of scientific approaches with naturopathy (which will be addressed later in relation to the threat posed by substitute products in the sector); (iii) innovation, conceived as a factor that encompasses the aforementioned elements and is constituted by collaboration among firms, understanding of customers' needs, objectives aimed at market penetration, and adaptability to change.

Analysis of Horizontal Competitive Forces

One of the risk factors for firms in the biotech sector is the threat posed by new entrants, *i.e.* the possibility that new or existing firms not yet active in the sector may enter the market and increase competition for the incumbent firms already established. The competitive pressure exerted by new entrants can produce different effects. For example, it may lead incumbent firms to modify the strategies they would have adopted in the absence of potential competitors, prompting them to undertake measures to deter entry or to increase investments to raise the costs and difficulties associated with market entry for other firms. The actual entry of new firms, however, depends on the extent of barriers, whether institutional, legal, structural, or strategic, that protect the sector from the introduction of new competitors. New entrants cannot enter under conditions equivalent to those faced by incumbents; therefore, a barrier to entry is any advantage possessed by firms already operating in the sector, and the magnitude of such advantage determines the height of the barrier (Caroli, 2021).

An example of a governmental authority that contributes to the establishment of legal and institutional barriers to entry in the sector within Europe is EMA. EMA is responsible for ensuring the scientific evaluation, oversight, and safety monitoring of medicines intended for both human and veterinary use throughout the European Union. Another example is the International Organization for Standardization (ISO), the foremost global organization responsible for developing and disseminating technical standards. These standards are highly relevant to the biotech sector and constitute an additional safeguard for the safety and quality of both products and services. Specifically, ISO 9001 is the international standard for quality management systems. This standard facilitates effective process control through systematic performance measurement and the identification of appropriate indicators. Furthermore, it supports the continuous pursuit of customer satisfaction by ensuring the consistent quality of goods and services over time (Way *et al.*, 2016). Furthermore, in this sector, particularly within the red biotech subsector, the World Health Organization (WHO) is highly relevant. It provides guidance on global health issues, directs health-related research, and establishes norms and standards concerning health policy decisions.

In addition to the institutional and legal barriers mentioned above, structural factors inherently limit the entry of new firms into the sector. For example, it can be considered the necessity of investing in R&D, for which quantitative data on the sector have already been presented, or the importance of shared process networks within the field of biotechnology (Jain, 2023; Wang & Yang, 2022). The aspects of knowledge sharing, networks, and open innovation promotion will be examined in greater detail in Chapter 2 (Ahn & Meeks, 2008; Johnson, Whittington & Scholes, 2014). The requirement for networking and collaboration could be considered an additional competitive force (Caroli, 2021) or be uniformly integrated into the sector's entry barriers. Entry into the sector can occur through three modalities. The first is the so-called go-alone approach, which entails direct entry and thus requires substantial initial investments by independent groups or emerging biotech firms. These are understood both as genuinely new or potential entrants to the sector and as firms operating in the red biotech subsector with a market capitalization below 10 billion dollars at the time of EMA approval. In this latter case, such firms are classified within the sector's existing competition rather than as new-entry threats. The second modality is collaboration, which constitutes the most effective, although complex, method of entry. Collaboration offers lower risk, reduced costs, and faster market integration. It involves the exploitation of one or more types of strategic partnerships that allow firms to associate before entering the sector or to collaborate with established biotech firms. The third modality is passive acquisition, whereby a firm is acquired by a group already incumbent in the sector (Deloitte, 2023). In addition to the risk of new entrants into the sector, another source of horizontal threat is represented by substitute products or services, *i.e.*, those that perform a similar function and therefore constitute valid alternatives to the products or services of the sector, even if they differ in features. The most evident alternative to biotechnological products appears to be natural products that do not rely on chemical or biological transformation methods (Shimasaki, 2020). As an example, within the red subsector, naturopathy can be considered. It offers natural therapies that are not included in conventional medicine protocols but are specifically defined as alternative. In fact, although sales of homeopathic products remain stable or are increasing globally, given the benefits many of these products offer to patients, they should nonetheless be considered complementary. Consequently, rather than detracting from the value of products within the biotech sector, they contribute to its overall enhancement.

In Europe, Traditional, Complementary and Integrative Medicine (TCIM) shows a certain degree of institutionalisation: in the WHO European Region, 23% of Member States report having a specific national policy for ICT, and 40% report having a national law or regulation on the subject. Therefore, despite the institutionalization and growth of the European market for homeopathic medicines and alternative and complementary medicine products, this does not seem to impact the competitiveness of the sector, as these products/services cannot be defined as viable alternatives to drugs or other biotechnological products (Zuzak *et al.*, 2013). Therefore, from a Porterian perspective, the competitive analysis of the sector indicates that horizontal competitive forces are relatively low for biotech firms.

Analysis of Vertical Competitive Forces

Vertical competitive forces are pressures that influence a firm's strategic behavior, upstream or downstream. The competitive pressure suppliers exert on firms in the biotech sector increases with suppliers' bargaining power. However, it should be clarified that this type of assessment provides only general indications. Indeed, the bargaining power of suppliers is best evaluated in the context of a specific relationship between two clearly identified parties. Given the ethical and social significance of the biotech sector (except for certain subsectors), it is important that all actors in the supply chain strive to deliver high-quality, safe ancillary materials (Wang & Jie, 2020). In the European life sciences sector, quality and safety aspects of supply are regulated by the Good Distribution Practices directive, which establishes minimum standards for suppliers to maintain the quality and integrity of medicinal products throughout the supply chain. This represents an example of a legal constraint that limits suppliers' power by imposing rather stringent guidelines that must be satisfied to avoid penalties or criminal proceedings.

As for the strategic factors influencing suppliers' bargaining power over firms in the biotech sector, several aspects should be considered. First, it should be mentioned that the possibility of internalizing supply processes. Such a possibility is limited by the complexity of producing the raw materials necessary for biotech firms, which would require investments in resources and expertise that are often unsustainable, not solely in economic terms. In addition, the number and characteristics of suppliers must be considered. Supplying firms are typically large-scale and highly specialized in production. A third aspect to be mentioned concerns the technical requirements of firms in the biotech sector and the characteristics of their products. These include rapid delivery and transportation times, extremely high-quality standards, meticulous attention throughout the production, distribution, and use phases, and the need for highly specialized and costly skills and resources for production. In light of the slight reduction in suppliers' bargaining power attributable to the mentioned legal constraints, nearly all the previously outlined factors exert a countervailing influence on competitive pressure, leading to a relatively high level of supplier bargaining power.

Shifting focus downstream, it is imperative to examine the bargaining power of customers of firms operating in the biotech sector, *i.e.*, the competitive pressure these customers can exert on the firms. To analyze this pressure, it is necessary, first and foremost, to identify the types of customers involved along with their specific characteristics. A distinctive feature of the biotech sector, particularly regarding the R&D business of firms, is that the multiplicity of clients is found within the B2B (business-to-business) grouping, meaning that the primary customers are other firms (Najafi-Tavani, *et al.*, 2023).

The following three considerations are useful for this aspect. First, all firms involved in highly advanced or specialized biotechnological production, for example, pharmaceuticals for the treatment of rare diseases, are minimally affected by inflation on raw materials or specific inputs, as they can transfer increased supply or production costs to their clients, who are typically large private firms requiring these products or public/governmental entities. Taking the example of medicines for rare diseases, the main buyers are public healthcare organizations, government assistance systems, or large private care institutions such as specialized centers for the treatment of specific pathologies, even outside the European context. This factor is evidenced, for instance, by the growth rate of medicine prices, which is often, if not always, higher than the average inflation rate. Given such a circumstance, the effect on clients' bargaining power is self-evident. When product specificity and complexity are high, as in the biotech sector, and when these products are essential to purchasing firms (*i.e.*, on the demand side), biotech firms have greater leverage over their clients. This reduces clients' bargaining power and increases biotech firms' bargaining power. A second consideration is that, very often, the supply contracts that buyers enter into with firms in the biotech sector do not allow clients to easily switch their biotech product suppliers, whether these are pharmaceuticals or other products (thus, switching costs are high). Furthermore, the low substitutability of these products, as noted in the analysis of horizontal competitive forces, further shifts bargaining power in favor of biotech firms rather than their clients. The third consideration is that most client firms in the sector are large firms that also handle product distribution, which, almost invariably, cannot be sold directly to end consumers (B2C) due to technical and logistical reasons (Skare, Gavurova & Rigelsky, 2023). These reasons include storage and transportation temperature requirements, challenges in downstream integration for many firms in the sector, and the creation and development of direct commercial channels, among others.

Overall, unlike upstream vertical competitive forces, customer pressure on firms in the biotech sector is not particularly strong. Nevertheless, given the inability to bypass or integrate intermediate distributors, who are the customers of firms within the sector, their bargaining power can be classified as medium to medium-high, depending on the specific grouping analyzed and the characteristics of the buyers.

In addition to the vertical competitive forces previously described, external competitive pressures affect firms in the biotech sector and influence the sector's overall attractiveness. Indeed, it has to be overlooked that the role of stakeholders other than customers and suppliers, *i.e.*, external stakeholders (Caroli, 2021; De Gooyert *et al.*, 2017; Freeman, Harrison & Wicks, 2007).

The first major category of external stakeholders to be considered is the scientific community, which serves both as a supplier and a customer to the biotech sector. On one hand, it provides knowledge, an essential "raw material" for the innovation of products and processes. On the other hand, it acts as a customer, as many outputs from firms in the sector serve as tools for the scientific community to advance research and studies in biotechnology. Another broad category of stakeholders, excluding primary suppliers and buyers, includes governmental and non-governmental institutions, regulatory agencies, and various commissions and bodies responsible for consumer protection. These entities monitor processes and ethical standards, ensuring that final products meet regulatory requirements before they are introduced to the market (Borge & Bröring, 2020). The larger the number, size, and institutional power of these external stakeholders, the lower the sector's attractiveness. In the context of biotechnology, without precisely quantifying stakeholder power, it can be asserted that these actors play a crucial role in safeguarding end consumers. This role benefits transparency and quality but tends to restrict the freedom and competitive space available to firms operating in the biotech sector.

EVIDENCE AND CURRENT DEVELOPMENTS IN THE SECTOR

To give some evidence and indicate the current developments in the sector, below is a focus on two European Countries: Spain and the UK.

Focus on Spain

To provide a comprehensive overview of the Spanish biotech sector, it is appropriate to refer to several of the principal findings from the most recent AseBio (2024) report, which may be organized into five overarching thematic areas.

First thematic area: composition of the sector. In 2021, a total of 4,362 firms were engaged in biotechnological activities. Among them, 898 were identified as real biotech firms. In that same year, the number of firms operating in the sector increased by 11.5 percent. Of these 898 firms, 54% were micro-firms or small firms, while 42% were medium-sized firms. Such a distribution pattern reflects a trend like that observed in the Italian sector, among the firms exclusively dedicated to biotechnology, 50% focused on human health, 39% on food-related applications, 15.4% on agricultural and forestry production, 13.5% on animal health and aquaculture, 11.2% on environmental applications, and 11.1% on industrial biotechnology.

Second thematic area: R&D investment. The levels of investment in R&D by biotech firms have shown a marked recovery, reaching 1.04 billion euros in 2021. This value represents an increase of 16% compared to the previous period, following the downturn caused by the pandemic and the ensuing public health crisis. Despite this rebound, the biotech sector has fallen to fifth position in the national ranking of R&D investment, now positioned behind the research, education, pharmaceutical, and automotive sectors.

Third thematic area: funding. In 2022, the volume of investment secured by Spanish biotech firms stabilized at 142 million euros, down from the total recorded in 2021. Crowdfunding is gaining traction as an alternative financing mechanism within the biotech sector, while equity investments by international institutions supporting firm development are emerging as a complementary avenue.

Fourth thematic area: collaboration and internationalization. Over the past five years, the number of collaborations has increased by nearly 50%. In total, biotech firms entered 295 partnerships, 66% of which were established with public sector organizations. Moreover, 31% of these agreements involved international counterparts, and 60% were specifically focused on R&D activities. In 2022, AseBio members expanded their international footprint by 20%, with 43 affiliated firms operating in 56 countries.

Fifth thematic area: impact on the national economy. The aggregate activity of biotech firms generated more than 11 billion euros in added value, representing 1% of Spain's GDP, and reported total turnover of nearly 13 billion euros, equivalent to 1.1% of GDP. The sector is among the few that recorded positive production growth, with biotech firms registering a 7.8% increase.

Although the agrifood biotech subsector is undergoing steady growth in Spain, the most scientifically significant firms are, for the most part, biopharmaceutical firms. Among these, Aelix Therapeutics merits particular mention. Aelix is a spin-off of HIVACAT, a Catalan program dedicated to the development of therapeutic vaccines and prevention strategies against HIV (Labiotech, 2023b), and is focused on developing a new therapeutic vaccine for HIV that may eventually be integrated into strategies for treatment and eradication (Bailón *et al.*,

2022). At the beginning of 2023, Aelix announced positive results from the AELIX-003 study, which assessed the safety, tolerability, immunogenicity, and efficacy of its vaccine in individuals living with HIV and on antiretroviral therapy. Alongside other international firms, Aelix forms part of an important research cluster that is striving to find a definitive solution to a challenge that has remained largely unresolved since 1981, the year in which the syndrome was first reported and when certain firms began to conduct studies into possible treatments and vaccines (Gottlieb *et al.*, 1981).

Another firm worth mentioning, although it cannot be strictly categorized within the red biotech sector, but rather belongs to the transversal subsector of services, is Chemotargets, a biotech firm founded in 2006 in Barcelona that specializes in assessing the efficacy and safety of novel drugs under development. The firm's CLARITY platform received licensing approval from the U.S. Food and Drug Administration (FDA) in response to the agency's requirement for a computational tool capable of predicting drug outcomes (Pharma Boardroom, 2022). Over time, Chemotargets has designed and continues to advance this integrated technological platform, CLARITY, which incorporates a wide range of cutting-edge computational methodologies to help clients expedite their drug discovery projects while improving cost efficiency. This platform is employed globally by a diverse array of experts, including chemists, biologists, pharmacologists, toxicologists, computational scientists, and regulators, and is utilized by both large and small pharmaceutical firms, as well as, notably, by the FDA's Center for Drug Evaluation and Research (FDA/CDER).

In summary, the analysis reveals that the Spanish biotech sector is experiencing growth, driven primarily by the activities of small and medium-sized firms predominantly operating in the health domain, with significant increases observed in R&D investments, international collaborations, and notable innovations such as those introduced by Aelix Therapeutics and Chemotargets.

Focus on the UK

The UK biotech sector has experienced significant growth, establishing itself as the European leader in both life sciences research and start-up financing. According to McKinsey's Biotech Innovation Index (McKinsey & Company, 2019, 2021), the UK excels in discovery, measured by scientific publications and patents, and in growth capital, including late-stage financing and public offerings, ranking immediately behind the USA globally. Nevertheless, strategic challenges persist in translating new knowledge into novel products and/or services. To enable comparability with the analysis conducted in the Spanish biotech sector, the same five macro-areas structure has been adopted (Hofer *et al.*, 2022).

First thematic area: composition of the sector. The UK boasts a rapidly expanding biotech sector, with a growing number of innovative firms operating across diverse areas of the life sciences. As of 2024, over 1,450 firms are active in the biotech sector with a focus on R&D (Statista, 2025a).

Second thematic area: R&D investment. The British government has introduced a new unified tax incentive scheme for R&D, granting a 20% credit on eligible R&D expenditures, which is treated as taxable income (BioIndustry Association, 2025). This scheme is designed to further encourage investment in R&D within the biotech sector (Nguyen & Turner, 2023).

Third thematic area: funding. In 2024, the UK biotech sector experienced substantial growth, raising 3.5 billion pounds in investment, a 94% increase from the previous year. This marks the highest annual investment figure since 2021, underscoring the sector's resilience, innovation, and global attractiveness despite difficult economic conditions.

Fourth thematic area: collaboration and internationalization. The British biotech sector demonstrated considerable resilience in the third quarter of 2024, securing a total of 808 million pounds in venture capital and public funding. This consistent flow of agreements highlights ongoing investor confidence in the sector's potential to drive innovation and stimulate growth. The UK continues to strengthen its position in the global biotechnology market, attracting significant investments from both domestic and international investors. The growing global appeal of the British biotech sector is evidenced by increased international investment and collaborations.

Fifth thematic area: impact on the national economy. The biotech sector constitutes a vital component of the British economy, contributing significantly to economic growth and employment. Government support, through tax incentives and R&D investments, underscores the sector's strategic importance to the national economy.

Within the British biotech sector, the most prominent firms also operate in the health domain (BioIndustry Association, 2018). Notably, GlaxoSmithKline (GSK), one of the world's leading pharmaceutical firms headquartered in Brentford, merits particular attention. Established in 2000 through the merger of Glaxo Wellcome and SmithKline Beecham, GSK operates across the pharmaceutical, vaccines, and consumer healthcare sectors. The firm is actively engaged in the R&D of new drugs and vaccines, thereby making a significant contribution to innovation across the biotechnology, pharmaceutical, and healthcare fields globally (GSK, 2025).

Immunocore, on the other hand, is a British biotech firm specializing in the development of innovative immunological therapies for the treatment of cancers and infectious diseases. The firm is renowned for its proprietary T-cell receptor (TCR) technology platform, which aims to harness the immune system's potential to recognize and combat diseased cells. Immunocore is publicly traded on Nasdaq and has a market capitalization of approximately $ 1.49 billion.

Prozomix Limited is a British biotech firm focused on intensive research and specialized in its proprietary genomic and metagenomic mining technology, GRASP. The firm is committed to discovering new biocatalysts for applications in biocatalysis and other emerging enzyme-related sectors.

Finally, the Jenner Institute is a research institute located in Oxford, established through a partnership between the University of Oxford and the British Institute for Animal Health. The institute specializes in vaccine development and the conduct of clinical trials for diseases such as malaria, tuberculosis, Ebola, and Middle East Respiratory Syndrome Coronavirus (MERS-CoV), thereby adopting a One Health approach. In 2020, it developed a COVID-19 vaccine in collaboration with the Italian firm Advent and the German group Merck.

In summary, the overview highlights the growth and importance of the UK's biotech sector, supported by significant investments, favorable government policies, and a strong appeal to international investors. The firms examined represent the UK's excellence in the biotech sector, contributing substantially to innovation and scientific research worldwide.

CONCLUDING REMARKS

The analysis of macro-environmental factors has underscored that, among the PESTEL factors, the political-institutional, technological, and legal factors are of strategic importance to European biotech firms. This does not mean that the economic, social, and environmental factors do not provide valuable insights for shaping decision-making processes, but rather that they are closely interconnected with the three categories mentioned. Indeed, political-institutional factors constitute the strategic framework within which new technologies (products and/or services) develop, ensuring compliance with European regulations while more effectively responding to current social and environmental needs.

The analysis of Michael E. Porter's five competitive forces reveals that the strategic characteristics defining the sector predominantly stem from its high growth rate. Indeed, this latter factor requires developing the capacity to access funding sources and attract investors, and to foster collaborative relationships with other players in the same or related sectors, particularly the pharmaceutical, healthcare, and academic sectors. In addition, it also requires promoting the development of innovative solutions (products, services, and/or processes) that simultaneously facilitate digitalization and gain access to distribution channels.

In addition to these, there is a need to situate firms within strategic areas (clusters) where multiple actors coexist and share value-creation processes. To date, European biotech firms are seeking new and interesting sources of value through a broad range of models and diversification strategies, including the development of potential blockbuster drugs and the exploration of next-generation therapies.

The biotech sector contributes substantially to Europe's knowledge-based economy. Therefore, investing in this sector is crucial to activating the engine of European innovation. Few sectors, such as biotech, can directly contribute to health and sustainable development while simultaneously generating virtuous cycles in investment, innovation, and employment.

CHAPTER 2

Managing Competition Through Strategic Collaborations

Abstract: This chapter analyzes the strategic importance of interorganizational collaborations in the biotech sector, emphasizing their role as key drivers of innovation and competitiveness in knowledge-intensive contexts. It first examines the theoretical and strategic dimensions of collaborative relationships, including their objectives, enabling conditions, governance mechanisms, and main organizational forms such as strategic alliances, research joint ventures, university–industry partnerships, networks, and innovation ecosystems. Attention is devoted to cross-sector collaborations involving biotechnology firms and organizations operating in pharmaceuticals, information technologies, agri-food systems, and academic research. These partnerships facilitate knowledge exchange, resource sharing, and risk distribution while supporting technological convergence and long-term value creation. The chapter also explores the strategic evolution of collaborations into mergers and acquisitions, which often represent a natural development of earlier partnerships. Through these processes, smaller biotech firms can capitalize on intellectual property and technological knowledge generated through collaborative projects, while larger corporations strengthen their innovation capabilities and expand their global competitive position. The chapter concludes that collaborations and acquisitions operate as complementary mechanisms for entrepreneurial renewal and sustainable competitiveness in the biotechnology industry.

Keywords: Cross-sector partnerships, Interorganizational collaborations, Mergers and acquisitions, Open innovation, Strategic alliances, Value creation.

INTRODUCTION

Competition at a global scale relies on the creation, acquisition, absorption, sharing, and transfer of new knowledge. Knowledge creation strongly influences the speed, quality, and quantity of innovation, while knowledge integration significantly impacts innovative performance. Firms strategically leverage innovation for three main reasons: to gain a competitive advantage, both locally and globally, to adapt their strategies to the evolving demands of the external environment, and, finally, to create value (Arsawan *et al.*, 2022). The propensity for innovation is greater in so-called knowledge-intensive sectors, such as pharmaceuticals, chemicals, biotechnology, electronics, telecommunications, and

Paola Olimpia Achard

information technology (Bloem & Salimi, 2023). Highly competitive sectors, such as biotechnology, tend to exhibit more cooperative interactions among firms.

The coexistence of competition and collaboration depends on a combination of sector-specific characteristics and the distinctive features of a firm's activities (primary and secondary). Relevant factors in the biotech sector include a high level of firm concentration (dichotomous structure; geographic clustering), along with the threat posed by potential new entrants. In addition, the presence of high entry barriers, including the need for large financial investments required for production and access to distribution channels (Fraterman, Wübbels & Kniss, 2023), as well as strategic barriers, should be considered. Finally, the ability of firms to build collaborative relationships is a key factor in determining their survival and long-term development. From a strategic perspective, the proliferation of collaborative strategies and strategic alliances for corporate governance is certainly one of the most compelling aspects of this sector.

The creation and dissemination of specialized knowledge, the containment of R&D costs, and the reduction of time-to-market are key competitiveness factors for European biotech firms. The transition from scientific discovery to market application represents a critical inflection point for biotech firms (Simon & Giovannetti, 2017). In this scenario, interorganizational collaborations (IORs) often arise to integrate complementary knowledge, share risks and capital, and develop solutions that would otherwise be unattainable with a single approach.

The present chapter aims to investigate strategic IORs in the biotech sector. To this end, it is divided into three sections. The first section introduces the strategic dimensions of IORs, highlighting their objectives, supporting factors and barriers, governance arrangements, and the typical forms of collaboration observed. The second section explores in greater depth the cross-sectoral dimension, illustrating its advantages, diffusion data, and several emblematic cases. Finally, the last section examines the evolution of collaborations into Merger & Acquisition (M&A) processes, presenting data and trends that underscore how such strategies are shaping the entire biotech ecosystem. A brief conclusion synthesizes the principal findings that have emerged, linking the analysis to the sector's future trends.

INTERORGANIZATIONAL COLLABORATIONS: RELEVANT STRATEGIC ELEMENTS

IORs represent a fundamental element for competitiveness and innovation across many sectors. In the biotech sector, characterized by high technological complexity and substantial R&D costs, these forms of collaboration play an even more critical role. The growing prevalence of alliances, joint ventures, and collaborative networks reflects the need to share resources, know-how, and the risks associated with developing innovative products and/or services (Achard & Bellini, 2023).

IORs are generally considered distinctive forms of interaction among two or more firms aimed at creating synergy that amplifies the scope and effectiveness of individual actors' strategies and behaviors (Taylor & Doerfel, 2005). Such a definition suggests that collaboration goes beyond mere cooperation and coordination (Gulati, Wohlgezogen & Zhelyazkov, 2012; Tee, Davies & Whyte, 2019). The development of IORs is particularly relevant for biotech firms in addressing the defining challenges of the macro-environment. These challenges include increasing healthcare demands associated with population aging, the growing incidence of chronic diseases, limited financial resources, the rapid pace of technological advancement, and heightened public expectations, particularly from informed and empowered citizens. From a strategic perspective, it is assumed that the cooperative choices of biotech firms are partly influenced by macro-environmental and sector-specific characteristics (see Chapter 1). Indeed, macro-environmental factors encourage biotech firms to pursue collaborative initiatives to enhance their governance capacity within competitive contexts. Furthermore, participation in collaborative networks is often motivated by firms' intention to expand their portfolios of distinctive resources and capabilities (Prahalad & Hamel, 1999), which can be leveraged to enhance innovation management. This highlights how strategic, collaborative interactions contribute to achieving biotech firms' strategic objectives.

Collaboration, in relation to a firm's competitive positioning, can manifest horizontally (within the same business area), vertically (along the production or supply chain), or laterally (between firms operating in different sectors or with diverse organizational types). In certain sectors, such as biotechnology, healthcare, and pharmaceuticals, there is a recognized coexistence of both competition and cooperation, a phenomenon referred to as co-opetition (Brandenburger & Nalebuff, 2011). Co-opetition depends on both the specific context and the nature of the activities involved. As a result, IORs can take a variety of forms, primarily shaped by the strategic needs and degree of horizontal integration among participating biotech and non-biotech firms.

Key issues related to IORs include, of course, the objectives behind the formation of strategic IORs, but also the factors that support the creation of IORs, the barriers that hinder their development, and, finally, the governance mechanisms and typologies that influence the structure of IORs. Compared to Gulati's perspective (Gulati, Wohlgezogen & Zhelyazkov, 2012) of collaboration as an umbrella term encompassing both cooperation and coordination, more recent studies (Kretschmer & Vanneste, 2017) recognize a clearer distinction between these constructs, while also emphasizing the need for further theoretical refinement.

Objectives

As said, several aspects are particularly relevant for IORs, including the objectives of the collaboration, the characteristics of the partners, enabling and constraining factors, governance mechanisms, and the forms of collaboration. The relative importance of these elements varies across the collaboration life cycle (Vurro *et al.*, 2024).

In the context of IORs, the objective, or set of objectives, represents the primary unit of analysis. These objectives can be private and/or collective in nature, and sometimes, even opportunistic in relation to other partners (Castañer & Oliveira, 2020). Five fundamental and potentially coexisting motivations underlying IORs can be identified: i) developing resources and skills; ii) improving effectiveness and efficiency; iii) expanding production and distribution capacity; iv) managing competition within the sector; and v) favoring emerging strategic approaches (Mintzberg, 1983). Indeed, firms engage in collaboration for a variety of purposes, which include developing innovations (Achard & Bellini, 2023; Hietala *et al.*, 2023; Khilji, Mroczkowski & Bernstein, 2006; Powell, Koput & Smith-Doerr, 1996; Smith, Sarabi, & Christopoulos, 2023), managing and transferring knowledge (Hetemi, Ordieres & Nuur, 2022), addressing grand challenges (Seidl & Werle, 2018; Steyer & Gilbert, 2013) and complex societal problems (Addy & Dubè, 2018), making supply chains more sustainable (Sharma *et al.*, 2022; Silva *et al.*, 2021), establishing standards (Leiponen, 2008), implementing creative (Windeler & Sydow, 2001) and complex projects (Chakkol, Selviaridis & Finne, 2018), responding to emergencies, creating value (Le Pennec & Raufflet, 2018), developing innovative solutions (Steyer & Gilbert, 2013) and increasing sustainable business management (Escher & Brzustewicz, 2020).

However, defining the purpose of the collaboration is not the only relevant aspect. Indeed, biotech firms should evaluate several key elements, which include the expected impact of the collaboration on each partner's strategic objectives and the balance between the costs and benefits arising from the agreement. Other key elements to be evaluated are the relationship's governance structure and the extent to which an appropriate balance between autonomy and integration is achieved within the alliance's management system. Therefore, it is worth analyzing these aspects in depth.

Supporting factors and barriers

The success of IORs depends on maintaining a balance between enabling factors and potential barriers (Achard, Bellini & Ioannucci, 2025). The drivers behind the creation of IORs arise from both macro-environmental pressures of a political and institutional nature that act as external catalysts, and from internal firm-level dynamics (de Jong *et al.*, 2023). Governments and healthcare institutions are among the main promoters of IORs, creating significant opportunities for biotech and non-biotech firms to engage in sophisticated learning processes aimed at developing more effective interorganizational collaboration processes (Breton *et al.*, 2013; Chalmers, Ashton & Tenbensel, 2017). In the case of biotech firms, additional external factors also include the geographic proximity to strategic organizations (*e.g.*, universities and research centers), which promote and support continuous learning, together with the presence of shared goals among the actors involved and the characteristics of the territorial context in which collaborations are established (Mervyn, Amoo & Malby, 2019).

Before examining the internal factors that drive collaboration within biotech firms, it is appropriate to consider two cross-cutting elements that significantly impact collaborative dynamics, *i.e.*, the participation of key actors in strategic planning and the availability of time-related resources. Regarding the first aspect, co-planning among participants enhances the effectiveness of interactions over time. Furthermore, it activates a virtuous cycle of knowledge transfer, in which competencies acquired through collaboration are shared across other areas of the firm. As for the second aspect, time emerges as a strategic resource in collaborative relationships. Indeed, time plays a key role in both the internal dynamics of the collaboration (synchronization between partners) and the alignment with the external context beyond the partnership (Oliveira, Lumineau & Ariño, 2023).

Academic literature has extensively explored the internal factors that foster the development of IORs (Kourti, 2021; Tran, 2023; Ziehe & Helfen, 2021). For instance, fostering organizational ambidexterity promotes collaborative processes by encouraging the sharing of objectives, resources, and activities (Lavikka, Smeds, & Jaatinen, 2015). Furthermore, the adoption of shared information systems, both at the intra-company level (Aulkemeier, Iacob & van Hillegersberg, 2019) and inter-company level (Radaelli, Spyridonidis & Currie, 2024), supports and facilitates collaboration. Access to data and the ability to use it for monitoring service quality are crucial for achieving shared strategic goals. In biotech firms, the sustainability of collaborative efforts is strongly influenced by the ability to foster interprofessional collaboration. Geographic, technological, and organizational proximity all positively influence coordination among participating actors (Otte-Trojel *et al.*, 2017).

While numerous external and internal factors stimulate the development of IORs to pursue both corporate and collective strategic objectives, it is equally important, especially in the biotech sector, to shed light on those factors that weaken the ability to engage effectively with other players. According to McKenzie & Smith Merry (2023), three main types of barriers can be identified: (i) financial (limited funding specifically allocated to collaborative initiatives), (ii) organizational (players' involvement), and (iii) governance-related (unclear distribution of responsibilities). Within organizational barriers, it is possible to distinguish ambiguity, complexity, and dynamism that characterize the formation of IORs between firms. In addition, in multi-stakeholder collaborations, these conditions can lead to dysfunctional decision-making, resulting in outcomes that deviate from the alliance's intended goals. A common example of decision-making dysfunctions in the biotech sector can be the fact that responsibility for the decision is passed back and forth among partners when a critical issue arises, or the fact that managers postpone decisions by deferring them to future meetings to avoid conflict, or that no one takes ownership for defining a clear plan of action or for responding to results.

Governance

The governance of IORs plays a crucial role in determining the effectiveness of collaborative efforts in achieving a collaborative competitive advantage. To this end, partner organizations must formalize their interactions and establish structured communication channels. In addition, they should plan training programs to strengthen collaborative skills and develop shared leadership (Hermans *et al.*, 2019). The dimensions of control and trust support effective IORs through the various phases of an IOR's life cycle (Hickey *et al.*, 2021). Interorganizational trust has been shown to exert a positive, significant, and direct effect on governance dimensions, including commitment, communication, interaction frequency, and coordination. These governance mechanisms, in turn, are strongly associated with improved innovation capacity and overall IOR success (Nguyen, Mai & Nguyen, 2023).

The ways in which collaborative interactions are governed determine the effectiveness and performance of IORs (Schepman *et al.*, 2018). It is therefore appropriate to distinguish between collaborative governance style, which refers to how collaboration is managed, and the governance of collaboration, which concerns the systems and structures that shape collaborative behavior. Specifically, IORs can be governed by leveraging either the actors involved, the structural configuration of the relationship (*i.e.*, the nature and intensity of interconnections among partners), or, finally, the collaborative processes themselves. A balanced attention to actors, structures, and processes is essential for ensuring governance, coordination, and effective allocation of resources (Vangen, Hayes & Cornforth, 2015).

Both contractual and relational forms of governance have a significant impact on players' collaboration across the entire life cycle of IORs, particularly in contexts involving innovation management (Liu & Ding, 2023).

Fig. (**9**) illustrates the conceptual multidimensional framework within which the analysis of IOR governance mechanisms is conducted (Roehrich *et al.*, 2020). The core concepts emerging from the framework are the environment, the interplay between relational and contractual governance, and performance outcomes. The arrows from outcomes to governance mechanisms suggest that actual performance outcomes in IORs, such as opportunistic behavior, inefficient exchanges, or underperforming relationships, can prompt adjustments in either contractual or relational governance structures. Some authors have also demonstrated that the intensity of IORs, both formal and informal, is a critical factor in achieving the strategic goals of collaboration (Chalmers Ashton & Tenbensel, 2017). Relationship intensity also introduces another important dimension: the form and nature of IORs.

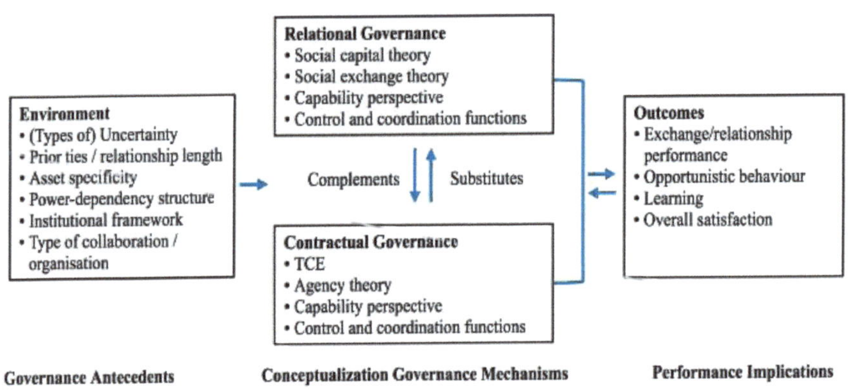

Fig. (9). Interorganizational Governance: a multidimensional framework (own elaboration, based on Roehrich *et al.*, 2020).

Possible Forms and Types of IORs

From a strategic perspective, the form of IOR is important because it depends on and is shaped by several previously discussed factors, namely the strategic objectives pursued, the firms involved, and the internal and external stimuli. Indeed, the potential success or effectiveness of IORs is based on the collaborative capacity of the firms involved. This capacity can be influenced by the relational capital held by the firms, the managerial style adopted, the clarity of strategic objectives, the organizational skills available, and the firm's reputation.

Over time, a specialized body of literature has emerged focusing on specific forms of IORs, such as strategic alliances (Vurro *et al.*, 2024), consortia (Yang, Zhang, & Zeng, 2022), international joint ventures (Nippa & Reuer, 2019), university-industry collaborations (Rybnicek & Königsgruber, 2019; Smith, Sarabi & Christopoulos, 2023; Zhou *et al.*, 2022), public-private partnerships (PPPs) (Steyer & Gilbert, 2013), networks and ecosystems (Shipilov & Gawer, 2020), regional clusters (Mitze & Strotebeck, 2019; Tallman *et al.*, 2004), and meta-organizations. In the case of biotech firms, the main forms of IOR (Achard & Bellini, 2023) include strategic alliances, research joint ventures, research consortia, university-industry partnerships, networks and clusters, and innovation ecosystems.

When discussing strategic alliances, it is impossible not to mention a major global event in which the biotech sector played a pivotal role: the COVID-19 pandemic. IORs, through strategic alliances, served as the primary vehicle for the rapid development of vaccines. A prominent example is BioNTech (Biopharmaceutical New Technologies), a fully integrated global firm founded in Germany in 2008, operating in the red biotech sector. Over time, BioNTech has established numerous partnerships with leading pharmaceutical firms, including Genmab, Sanofi, Genentech, Regeneron, Genevant, Fosun Pharma, and Pfizer (Pfizer, 2025). The strategic alliance with Pfizer enabled BioNTech to develop, produce, and commercialize the first FDA-approved mRNA vaccine and the first COVID-19 vaccine. In more detail, the collaboration began in March 2020 and was built upon a pre-existing partnership established in 2018 for the development of an mRNA influenza vaccine. Following the scientific success of the first COVID-19 vaccine, the two firms entered into a new agreement to facilitate the development and commercialization of an mRNA vaccine for the prevention of shingles.

Research Joint Ventures, on the other hand, are a form of IOR that helps overcome potential gaps between R&D policies, the free dissemination of knowledge, private incentives to invest in R&D, and profit appropriation (Cassiman, Veugelers & Arts, 2018). A particularly interesting case is that of Xellbiogene, a firm dedicated to the development and production of biologics and advanced therapies for the treatment of oncological and hematological diseases, for research institutions, pharmaceutical firms, hospitals, and charitable organizations. The firm was founded as a joint venture between two private institutions operating within the Italian National Health System: the Bambino

Gesù Children's Hospital and the Agostino Gemelli University Hospital Foundation (Osservatorio Malattie Rare – OMAR, 2025).

Knowledge transfer between academia and industry (university-industry partnerships) can be seen as a key driver of innovation and economic growth. It requires two-way knowledge sharing to identify relevant issues, share and develop new insights, and facilitate the transfer and implementation of knowledge and technologies (de Wit-de Vries *et al.*, 2019). An Italian example is the joint-stock firm EryDel, a spin-off of the University of Urbino (Uniurb, 2025). EryDel operates in the field of red biotechnology and develops innovative medical technologies. It has attracted over €30 million in funding from venture capital funds and European loans. Its primary objective is to commercialize the EryDex System medical device, currently in Phase III clinical development, to improve the management of ataxia telangiectasia, a rare genetic disease. The firm continues its strategic collaboration with the University for the industrial and clinical development of research results originating from the University's laboratories.

Firms participating in R&D consortia (networks) can not only reap the usual benefits of cooperation but also foster communication and mutual learning by sharing knowledge with other consortium members (Yang, Zhang & Zeng, 2022). A notable example is the Biobased Industries Consortium (BIC), which includes over 240 firms spanning all stages of the value chain (BIC, 2025). The Consortium's strategic objective is to promote the creation of a sustainable bioeconomy in Europe. BIC members operate in both green and blue biotechnologies, as well as in other complementary sectors. The Consortium is also a private partner in the Circular Bio-based Europe Joint Undertaking (CBE JU), a €2 billion public-private partnership (PPP) with the European Commission.

Regional clusters benefit from the positive competitive effects generated by IORs, as well as from more favorable access to funding sources (Olk & West, 2020). Furthermore, according to Delgado, Porter, & Stern (2014), multiple types of externalities occur, including knowledge, skills, and input-output linkages. An interesting example of regional clusters can be found in the Emilia-Romagna Region (central Italy), where seven so-called Clust-ERs operate to enhance the competitiveness of firms operating in various sectors, including healthcare, building and construction, culture and creativity, energy and sustainability, service innovation, and mechatronics and motors. Clust-ERs are part of the regional innovation network coordinated by ART-ER (Attractiveness Research Territory). Clust-ER Health is an association composed of large and small firms, laboratories from the High Technology Network, research centers, healthcare facilities, and training institutions. These actors share skills, ideas, and resources to enhance the regional healthcare system's competitiveness. The business areas are related to red biotechnologies. Clust-ER Health represents a key player in the regional innovation ecosystem and contributes to territorial development through a collaborative approach (Clust-ER, 2025).

Finally, innovation ecosystems (Granstrand & Holgersson, 2020) refer to the evolving set of actors, activities, artifacts, institutions, and relationships, including both complementary and substitutive interactions, that are essential to the innovative performance of a single actor or a population of actors. A representative European example is IBISBA (2025), a pan-European research infrastructure dedicated to gene-based bio-based industries (white biotechnology). IBISBA brings together leading European public research facilities from 10 countries to support the development of low-carbon, low- impact solutions. This ecosystem accelerates the generation and translation of cutting-edge knowledge into innovation by enabling the sharing of expertise and R&D facilities.

The importance of the mentioned relationships lies in the fact that IORs accelerate the flow of resources and expertise, particularly in production and R&D activities. The proliferation of various forms of collaboration reflects macro-environmental and sectoral characteristics, highlighting how innovative pathways can be pursued through the activation of IORs. Cooperative environments serve as potential platforms for both indirect and direct knowledge transmission. A systematic review of the literature on the role of cooperation in innovation efforts confirms that IORs have a positive impact on innovation performance (Freire & Gonçalves, 2022). In fact, innovation can only occur in the presence of knowledge sharing (Kremer, Villamor, & Aguinis, 2019). Firms that actively encourage knowledge sharing enhance their innovation capabilities (Castañeda & Cuellar, 2020). The strategic relevance of IORs stems from their contribution to value creation. Biotech firms engaged in collaborative efforts generate innovation, fostering value creation.

CROSS-SECTOR COLLABORATIONS AS A WAY OF VALUE CREATION

As in all knowledge-intensive sectors, biotech firms face significant challenges due to the high complexity of R&D activities, long project life cycles, and substantial investment requirements. To address these challenges and maintain a competitive edge, an increasing number of biotech firms are entering into IORs with organizations across sectors (*e.g.*, pharmaceuticals, ICT, cosmetics, agri-food). Cross-sector relationships (Fig. **10**) are particularly significant in R&D activities, where the need for specialized expertise and substantial capital makes resource sharing among multiple partners highly advantageous. Indeed, these alliances enable firms to combine complementary resources and expertise, access new knowledge, overcome technological barriers, and develop innovations that transcend the boundaries of a single sector. Moreover, the diversification resulting from such collaborations reduces economic and financial dependence on a single business area, mitigating risks and fostering long-term value creation.

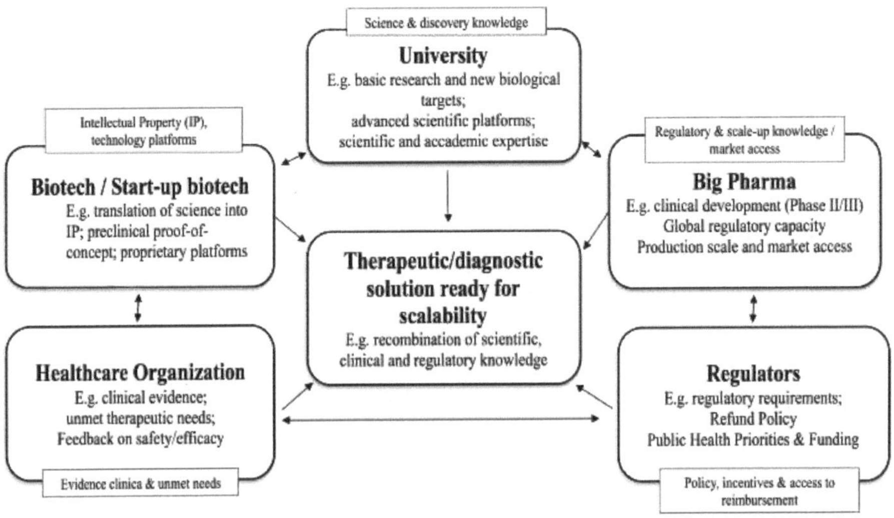

Fig. (10). Cross-sector collaboration as an infrastructure for the exchange of knowledge in innovation (own elaboration, based on Chesbrough, 2003; Etzkowitz & Leydesdorff, 2000; Powell, Koput, & Smith-Doerr, L. 1996).

The analysis of cross-sector collaborations established by biotech firms highlights convergence dynamics across disciplines and underscores the importance of open innovation and knowledge sharing. On one hand, biotech firms benefit from external investments and expertise to accelerate progress in scientific and technological research; on the other hand, partner organizations leverage biotechnology know-how to diversify their product and service offerings. As field research has shown, the success of such collaborations largely depends on firms' ability to coordinate projects and resources effectively and to overcome the cultural and organizational differences typical of heterogeneous industrial environments. Consequently, cross-sector collaborations are a key driver of innovation and competitiveness in the biotech sector, as they enable the exploitation of synergies in knowledge, funding, and access to new markets. When managed appropriately, these partnerships not only lead to product and process innovations but also contribute at a strategic level by fostering interdisciplinary skills, reducing risk, and facilitating entry into high-potential business areas.

Advantages and Strategic Motivations for Cross-Sector Collaborations

The findings derived from the analysis of the macro-environment and competitive dynamics of the European biotech sector are further supported by the study of literature trends. Fig. (**11**) clearly shows the growing, albeit uneven, proliferation of scientific publications on this topic over the past few years.

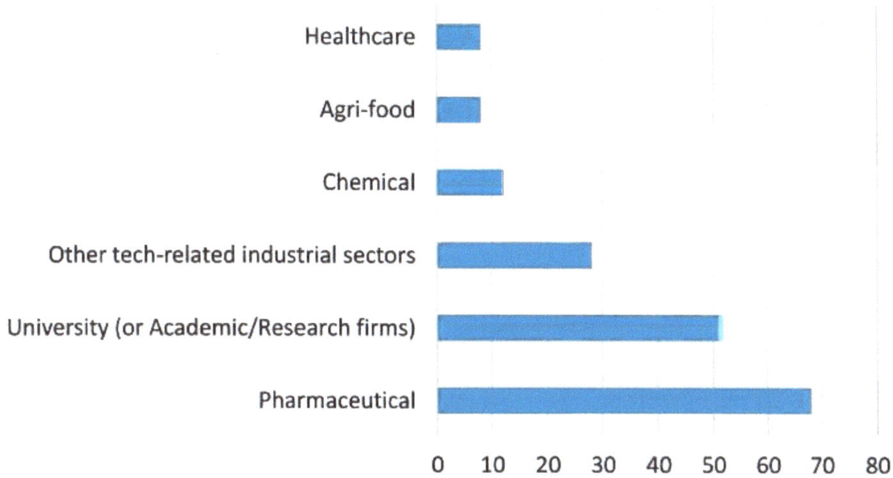

Fig. (11). Number of documents retrieved per year (1997-2024) (own elaboration).

Fig. (**12**), instead, presents the percentage of selected academic papers discussing collaborations between biotech firms and firms from various sectors. Many of these studies examine partnerships involving two or more sectors in addition to biotechnology. Notably, nearly seven out of ten papers analyze collaborations between biotech and pharmaceutical firms, while more than half (52%) focus on partnerships between biotech firms and universities or research centers. It is important to clarify that the technology-related industrial sectors referenced in Fig. (**12**) include, among others: telecommunications, ICT, digital technologies, AI, automotive, medical technology, and other high-tech sectors.

Cross-sector collaborations in the biotech sector primarily arise from strategic considerations. Biotech firms, which face high R&D costs and often extended development timelines, view these alliances as opportunities to access expertise and resources that would otherwise be difficult to acquire quickly. Sharing investments and knowledge reduces overall risk for all parties involved and enables firms to pursue more ambitious innovation trajectories. Additionally, diversifying their activities by engaging with different sectors provides an effective strategy for mitigating market uncertainties, spreading costs across multiple projects, and opening new revenue streams.

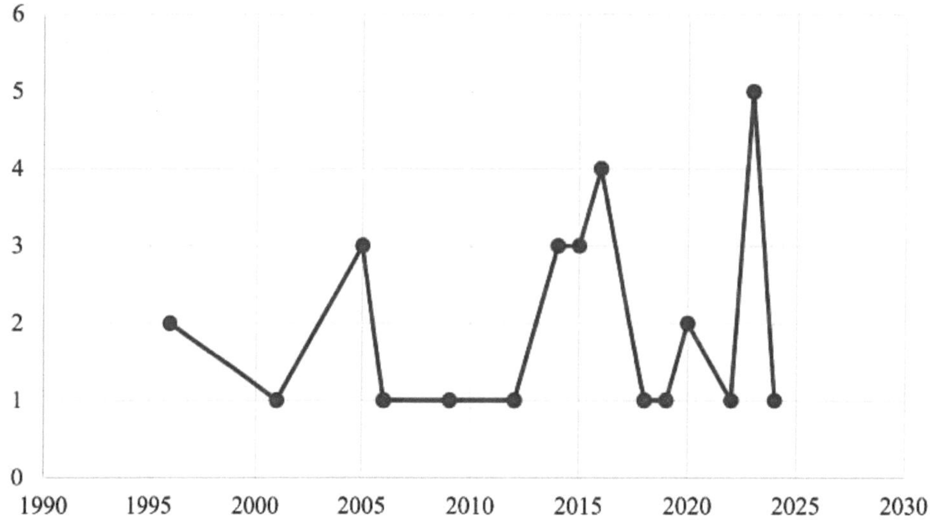

Fig. (12). Selected documents grouped by sector involved in the collaborations studied (own elaboration).

Cross-sector collaborations are also structured around specific activities within the value chain, depending on the needs and expertise required. Typically, the initial point of convergence is R&D, where the complexity of scientific research and the need for costly infrastructure are more effectively addressed through cooperation with partners offering complementary capabilities. Subsequent stages, including clinical trials, large-scale production and scaling, marketing, and distribution, also demand expertise and infrastructure that biotech firms may not possess internally. In such cases, collaborations with pharmaceutical or chemical firms, established distribution networks, or healthcare providers become essential to transforming innovation into marketable products. It is therefore unsurprising that partners originate from a wide range of sectors. The pharmaceutical sector, traditionally closely aligned with biotechnology activities, remains predominant. However, ICT and high-tech firms are becoming increasingly relevant in the digital age, while the agri-food and cosmetics sectors view biotechnology research as a source of next-generation solutions and products. Universities and research centers also play a crucial role and are often regarded as strategic partners for developing advanced technologies and training highly specialized personnel.

In terms of time horizon, collaborations focused on research and innovation typically span the medium- to long-term, as the development cycles for biotechnology products and processes can last several years, encompassing feasibility studies, laboratory testing, and regulatory approval processes. In contrast, agreements centered on commercial or distribution objectives tend to be shorter-term, often designed to achieve immediate goals such as rapid market entry or the swift promotion of a new product. Even in these cases, however, a modular approach is sometimes adopted, launching pilot projects to test the compatibility between partners, the stability of the agreement, and ultimately the viability of an initiative that could evolve into a more enduring collaboration.

Challenges and Managerial Implications

Cross-sector collaborations in biotechnology present several challenges that, if not adequately addressed, can compromise their overall effectiveness. The most important one is the need for organizational coordination. Firms operating in different sectors must manage work plans, tangible and intangible resources, and diverse teams, often distributed across multiple locations or countries, making effective planning and transparent communication systems essential. Another important challenge is the potential for cultural and strategic divergences. Organizations may differ in values, corporate cultures, processes, languages, and visions, and if these are not harmonized, they can lead to misunderstandings, misaligned objectives, and project delays. Finally, a third crucial issue concerns IP protection. The methods for exploiting patents, licenses, and proprietary know-how must be clearly defined to protect both the owners of the technology and those investing resources in its application. Equally important is the concept of absorptive capacity, that is, a firm's ability to recognize the value of new external knowledge, assimilate it, and apply it to commercial ends. Without this capacity, collaboration risks becoming a superficial exchange of ideas with limited impact on actual processes, products, or services. At the same time, such partnerships can yield significant benefits. For biotech firms, cross-sector collaboration often enhances innovation capacity. The cross-fertilization of approaches and expertise from different fields can stimulate creativity and accelerate the development of radical or incremental solutions. This may lead to a faster time-to-market, as shared infrastructure, pooled resources (including financial capital), and broader commercial networks help overcome obstacles that would typically delay progress for a single firm. Furthermore, adopting a collaborative strategic approach facilitates cost-sharing, often critical in R&D-intensive contexts, and mitigates risk. A larger pool of partners and capital promotes economies of scale and distributes financial burdens more equitably.

Synergies between biotechnology and other sectors can also open access to previously untapped markets, expanding product and service portfolios, and diversifying opportunities for long-term growth and business resilience. In conclusion, biotech firms, driven by the complexity of their competitive environment and the knowledge-intensive nature of their activities, are increasingly turning to strategic cross-sector collaborations to enhance their innovation potential.

While academic literature has thoroughly explored university–industry partnerships, there remains a significant gap in the study of collaborations with firms from other sectors, which often offer equally promising synergies. The value of cross-sector collaborations lies not only in generating competitive advantage but also in serving as a lever for innovation and long-term value creation, in line with the principles of open innovation and the insights of Powell, Koput & Smith-Doerr (1996) on the role of collaborative networks.

Sectoral heterogeneity introduces specific challenges. On the one hand, it demands that biotech firms adopt partnership management practices oriented toward knowledge and resource sharing. On the other hand, it requires diversification strategies that balance long-term investments in highly regulated sectors (*e.g.*, pharmaceuticals) with more agile operations in less complex markets (such as cosmetics or nutraceuticals). Reducing cultural and organizational gaps is also essential and can be supported through joint training programs, clearly defined decision-making procedures, and pilot projects to progressively test partner compatibility.

Looking ahead, the growth of cross-sector collaborations will likely be influenced by three key drivers: the adoption of digital technologies, which can streamline communication and coordination; the increasing convergence across related sectors, which lowers barriers along the value chain; and the growing emphasis on sustainability criteria, which will impact both partner selection and the nature of innovation initiatives. By consciously leveraging these trends, biotechnology managers can design and develop cross-sector collaborations that significantly strengthen their competitiveness and adaptability amid constant market evolution.

STRATEGIC EVOLUTION OF COLLABORATIONS: MERGERS & ACQUISITIONS

The collaborative strategies previously discussed enable biotech firms to share risk and expertise, accelerate innovation, and access new market opportunities. Over time, however, the need to consolidate competitive positioning and maximize return on investment may lead to more structured forms of integration, culminating in Mergers and Acquisitions (M&A). M&A represents the natural evolution of collaborative processes. On one side, large firms (*e.g.*, pharmaceutical firms) can strengthen their research pipelines by acquiring technologies and expertise developed by smaller biotech firms. On the other hand, these smaller firms can implement exit strategies that monetize the value created through earlier partnerships. This downstream integration approach not only shortens time-to-market but also reduces the uncertainty typically associated with long development cycles for drugs and biotechnology products. In this context, factors such as capital availability and the strength of prior collaborative networks can significantly accelerate the transition from strategic alliances to M&A deals. From a managerial perspective, the phases leading to full integration must be carefully planned, starting with initial collaboration agreements and IP frameworks, to ensure readiness for future mergers or acquisitions. The synergies that arise from a unified corporate structure in terms of resources, technologies, and market access must be balanced by effective organizational change management to avoid the dilution or loss of core competencies. Ultimately, M&A represents a critical step for biotech firms seeking to consolidate their market position or execute business exit strategies, fully realizing the value generated through earlier cross-sector collaborations.

Mergers & Acquisitions as Exit Strategies

Within the biotech sector, M&A represents by far the most common exit strategy (or entrepreneurial exit strategy), significantly more prevalent than Initial Public Offerings (IPOs), as illustrated in Figs. (**13** and **14**).

The high frequency of M&A can be attributed to several structural characteristics of the sector, such as lengthy R&D processes, the need for substantial financial resources, regulatory complexity, and the high risk of project failure. Under these conditions, small and medium-sized biotech firms often view M&A as a relatively fast and viable solution to monetize their knowledge, patents, and product pipelines. In exchange, acquiring firms, typically large pharmaceutical firms or corporate groups operating in multiple technology-intensive sectors, gain access to innovation, specialized expertise, and new growth opportunities.

Fig. (13). Dissemination of M&A and IPO strategies in the global biotech sector (2024) (own elaboration).

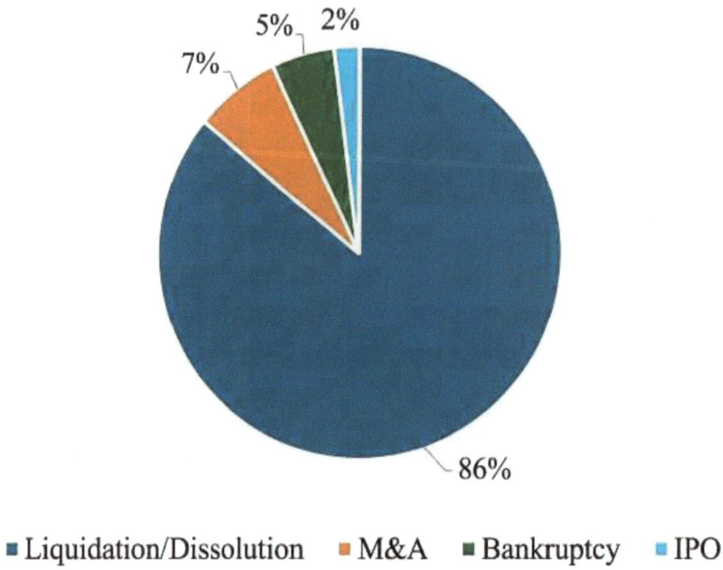

Fig. (14). Exit typologies distribution - Italian biotech sector (data from 2002 to 2024) (own elaboration).

One key reason M&A is preferred over other growth strategies is the immediate cash flow that it can generate for the target biotech firm. In contrast, an IPO involves extensive preparation, including drafting detailed prospectuses and strict regulatory compliance. An acquisition, by comparison, allows for quicker ownership transfer and a more certain financial return. Large pharmaceutical firms, continuously seeking innovative solutions to expand their product portfolios, are especially interested in biotech firms that have already demonstrated the scientific validity of their research, whether through lab studies or advanced clinical trials. Even if a product is not yet ready for market launch, what matters is the project's potential and the presence of proprietary patents or non-replicable know-how. The convergence between the biotech and pharmaceutical sectors ("bio-to-pharma") is among the clearest examples of how M&A fosters technology and knowledge transfer. Biotech firms, often highly research-oriented, focus on disruptive innovation, while big pharma brings the resources needed to conduct large-scale clinical trials, navigate regulatory systems, and access global markets. The combination of these strengths creates mutually beneficial synergies. The biotech firm monetizes its innovation, and the multinational pharmaceutical firm strengthens its pipeline and competitive edge. This explains the prevalence of so-called vertical M&As, in which the acquiring firm integrates upstream biotechnology capabilities to develop more comprehensive downstream solutions.

From a strategic standpoint, M&A is typically analyzed in terms of both short-term objectives and long-term opportunities. In the short term, a firm might acquire a mature biotech firm close to product or technology launch, thereby realizing immediate gains. Conversely, some acquiring firms invest in early-stage startups with highly innovative ideas in emerging areas like personalized medicine or gene therapies, betting on long-term value. This approach provides access to groundbreaking technologies, albeit with the understanding that additional investment and development time will be required before commercial viability is achieved.

M&A is not merely a financial transaction; it also involves complex organizational and cultural integration. In many bio-to-pharma acquisitions, the biotech firm retains some managerial and operational autonomy, functioning as an internal innovation hub under the parent firm's umbrella. This strategy helps preserve the agility and creativity that characterize small, innovative firms, which might otherwise be stifled by the more rigid structures of large corporations. In other cases, deeper integration culminates in a full merger. In these scenarios, the challenge is to retain the core competencies that made the biotech firm attractive while aligning it with the corporate-level strategies of the portfolio.

Another critical dimension is the relationship between M&A and entrepreneurial dynamism. Numerous studies show that the acquisition of biotech firms can lead to "entrepreneurial recycling," in which the founders, researchers, and managers of the acquired firm reinvest capital and expertise to launch new ventures. This dynamic strengthens the innovation ecosystem: knowledge circulates, new ideas are born, and the sector becomes more competitive. From this perspective, M&A also serves as a driver of local and national entrepreneurial development, offering tangible returns on entrepreneurial risk and encouraging new investment.

Among the factors that facilitate M&A are macro-environmental conditions such as R&D expenditure, the presence of technology clusters, regulatory stability, and financial system openness, as illustrated in Fig. (**15**). Countries and regions that invest heavily in R&D through both public and private channels, tend to be more attractive to investors, offering a rich talent pool, suitable infrastructure, and a strong academic foundation (*e.g.*, universities, research centers). Likewise, the possibility of establishing partnerships with industrial and institutional players enhances a biotech firm's market credibility and can make it more appealing to potential acquirers. Nonetheless, post-acquisition risks should not be underestimated. The reallocation of personnel and the potential loss of key talent (*e.g.*, lead researchers or decision-makers) can threaten project continuity unless effective retention plans are put in place. Cultural differences between a small, research-driven firm and a large, multinational organization may also lead to internal conflict, hindering decision-making and slowing down R&D progress. Indeed, some research highlights how an excessive focus on financial metrics, without adequate attention to organizational dynamics, can compromise the intended benefits of M&A, particularly in terms of innovation outcomes.

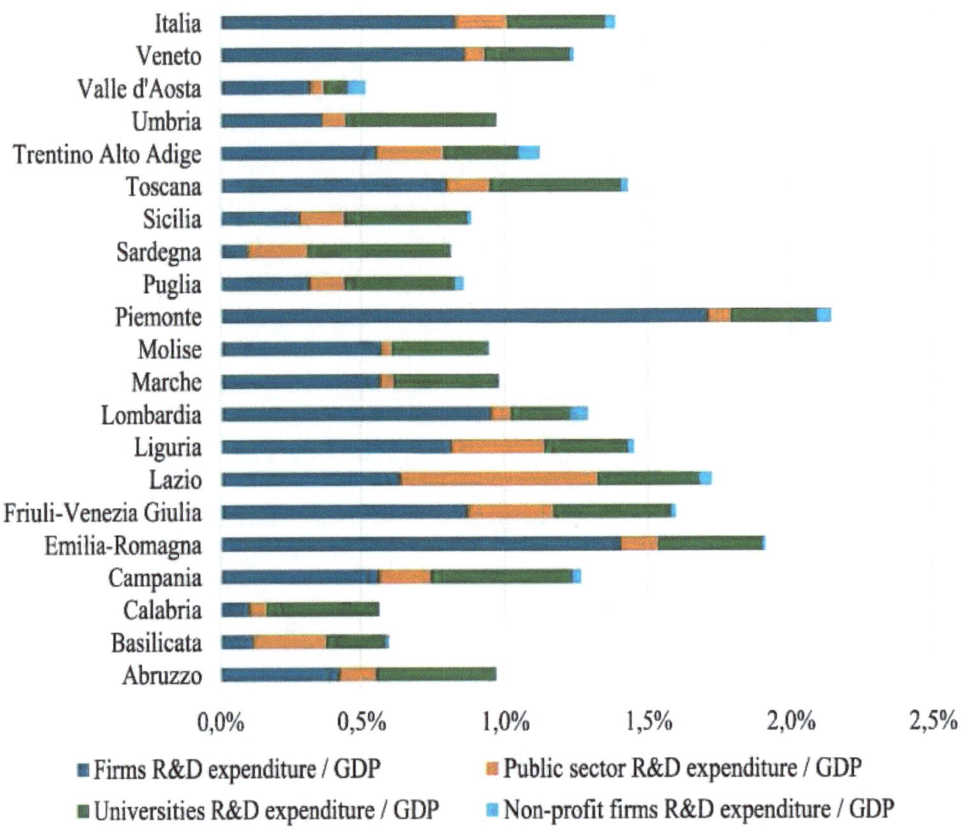

Fig. (15). Innovation in Italy: macro-environmental factors (own elaboration).

Overall, M&A remains the preferred strategy for monetizing the IP property and knowledge developed by biotech firms, while also enabling access to capital and complementary expertise. Indeed, they provide a more direct, industry-grounded path to market. This is particularly relevant in contexts where biotech startups and SMEs are abundant but lack the resources to independently manage the final stages of product development and commercialization. For the selling firm, M&A offers the opportunity to divest and reinvest capital in new ventures. For the acquiring firm, it provides access to patents, technologies, and know-how that close internal innovation gaps or reinforce existing capabilities. This synergy is increasingly important in an era of rapid scientific advancement, where firms in the pharmaceutical, chemical, and related sectors must maintain continuously updated project portfolios to meet evolving healthcare, environmental, and industrial needs.

Table 4. Examples of Bio-to-pharma M&As (own elaboration).

M&A (year)	Size (B$)	Core technology	Strategic rationale	Integrated knowledge	Competitive impact
Roche – Spark (2019)	4,3	AAV gene therapy	Secure a validated ATMP platform and expand into genetic ophthalmology	Regulatory expertise. AAV vector GMP production	Become a leader in gene therapy
Amgen – Horizon (2022)	27,8	Autoimmune and rare inflammatory diseases	Reinforce the portfolio prior to the major patent expires.	Ultra-specialized clinical development and immunology know-how	Immediate revenue accretion and mitigation of post-cliff exposure
Merck – Prometheus (2023)	10,8	Precision medicine platform for IBD	Leverage a scalable biomarker platform for cross-indication expansion.	Biomarker discovery, translational analytics	Become a long-term leadership in immunology
Pfizer – Trillium (2021)	2,3	CD47-targeted immuno-oncology	Acquire differentiated IO research and deepen next-gen immunotherapy portfolio.	Tacit antibody design and Fc-engineering expertise	Strengthens Pfizer's IO bench and complements existing oncology franchises
Novartis – Avidity (2025)	12	AOC™ RNA conjugates	Secure proprietary RNA-delivery technology	Rare disease clinical execution	Become a frontrunner in RNA therapeutics

The set of transactions reported in Table **4** illustrates how bio-to-pharma M&A does not function merely as a mechanism for simple scale expansion. It can be considered more as a tool for targeted capability acquisition and knowledge recombination. Across the Roche - Spark, Amgen - Horizon, Merck - Prometheus, Pfizer – Trillium, and Novartis - Avidity M&As, several common patterns emerge, alongside important differences in clinical maturity, technological risk profile, and competitive intent. Indeed, all five cases are consistent with the notion of markets for technology (Arora, Fosfuri & Gambardella, 2001). The acquirers are not buying revenue streams or sales infrastructures, but pre-assembled bundles of technology, know-how, and regulatory experience.

The Roche - Spark and Novartis - Avidity transactions, for example, are emblematic of acquisitions in which the main asset is a platform technology (respectively, AAV gene therapy and AOC RNA conjugates), rather than a single product. Similarly, Merck - Prometheus and Pfizer - Trillium target platform-like capabilities in precision immunology and next-generation immuno-oncology, which can be deployed across multiple indications over time.

All five examples contribute to reshaping the acquirer's competitive position along future technological trajectories. Amgen uses Horizon to immediately strengthen its autoimmune and rare disease franchise and smooth the revenue curve post–patent cliff, whereas Roche leverages Spark to secure an early leadership position in gene therapy and rare inherited retinal diseases. Merck's acquisition of Prometheus is explicitly about precision medicine in immunology, reflecting a strategic intent to move from broad immunomodulators to biomarker-driven patient stratification. Pfizer's acquisition of Trillium, focused on CD47 and IO research, deepens its bench in a highly contested field where differentiation increasingly depends on novel mechanisms of action. Novartis, in turn, uses Avidity to reconfigure its post-2030 neuromuscular pipeline, anchoring its long-run growth to RNA-based modalities. In all instances, the deals aim to reposition the acquirer in future technology–market "spaces" rather than merely reinforcing current competitive positions (Teece, 2007; Teece, Pisano & Shuen, 1997).

A cross-case comparison also highlights that the type of knowledge being integrated is predominantly tacit, system-level capability, not just codified IP. The table explicitly shows that the acquisition includes regulatory expertise, GMP production know-how, ultra-specialized clinical development capabilities, bioinformatics and biomarker discovery skills, antibody design heuristics, and rare-disease clinical execution. This aligns closely with the literature on absorptive capacity (Cohen & Levinthal, 1990) and knowledge stickiness (Szulanski, 1996). Such capabilities are difficult to transfer *via* contractual collaborations alone, because they are deeply embedded in routines, teams, and organizational processes (Nonaka, Takeuchi & Umemoto 1996). M&A, in these cases, is the governance mechanism that enables internalizing these capabilities and reorganizing them within the acquirer's own architecture (Nickerson & Zenger, 2004).

Viewed through the lens of dynamic capabilities, the reported cases exemplify the triad of sensing, seizing, and reconfiguring (Teece, 2007). All the considered big-pharma sense emerging technological trajectories (gene therapy, RNA therapeutics, precision immunology, next-gen IO, rare disease platforms) by monitoring the biotech ecosystem and its scientific frontiers. In addition, all of them seize those opportunities by structuring large-scale M&A transactions that internalize crucial platform technologies and associated know-how at specific windows of time (before competitors move or asset valuations become prohibitive). Finally, all of them reconfigure their internal resource base by integrating the acquired platforms into existing R&D, regulatory, and commercial infrastructures, often redefining their therapeutic focus and long-term portfolio strategy.

As said, of course, there are also several differences in how strongly each deal leans toward exploration versus exploitation. Amgen - Horizon has a comparatively stronger exploitation component: integrating marketed and late-stage assets to sustain cash flows and defend against revenue erosion. Pfizer - Trillium, Merck – Prometheus, and Novartis - Avidity are more heavily tilted toward exploration, as they absorb early- and mid-stage platforms whose primary value lies in opening new technological options. Roche - Spark sits in the middle, combining an approved product with highly exploratory platform potential. This blend of exploratory and exploitative motives mirrors the concept of organizational ambidexterity (O'Reilly & Tushman, 2013), in which incumbents must simultaneously sustain current earnings and prepare for discontinuous technological shifts.

Another salient pattern concerns systemic complementarities and modularity. All five transactions occur in domains where the value of any single component (*e.g.*, a vector, an RNA chemistry, a biomarker algorithm) depends heavily on the availability of complementary assets (production, clinical networks, regulatory credibility, data infrastructures) that large incumbents are better positioned to provide (Brusoni, Prencipe & Pavitt, 2001; Pisano, 2006). From this perspective, the M&A move can be seen as the point where distributed, partially modular science is reassembled into a coherent industrial architecture (Baldwin & Clark, 2000; Henderson & Clark, 1990).

The mentioned cases collectively suggest a model in which biotech firms operate as highly specialized exploratory nodes within a broader innovation network, while big pharma incumbents act as platform integrators and global scale-up engines (Owen-Smith & Powell, 2004; Powell *et al.*, 2005). M&A is the moment in which the exploratory, networked innovation of biotechnology is translated into industrial, global, and reimbursable therapies. The comparative analysis thus reinforces the previously mentioned concept that, in the biotech sector, M&A is best understood not as a financial exit, but as a structured mechanism for the reallocation, recombination, and scaling of knowledge across the industry-wide innovation system.

CONCLUDING REMARKS

Strategic IORs in the biotech sector are emerging as a fundamental pillar of innovation and competitiveness, particularly considering the scientific complexity, high R&D costs, and regulatory challenges that define the external environment. Collaboration enables the sharing of resources and expertise, reducing risk and allowing firms to better respond to growing demand for high-tech solutions. The importance of these alliances is reflected in a variety of collaborative models, ranging from small-scale research consortia to full-scale M&A, where the integration of competencies and production assets provides immediate competitive consolidation. Given the sector's long and costly development cycles, collaboration is not merely a strategic option, but a crucial vehicle for value creation and competitive advantage through the exchange of know-how. Cross-sector alliances offer opportunities to combine expertise from different (often interdisciplinary) fields, accelerating innovation and enabling the development of novel solutions. However, such alliances require effective coordination, the protection of IP, and a careful balance between autonomy, accountability, and integration. In some cases, collaboration evolves into M&A when biotech firms reach a level of maturity that makes them attractive to larger groups. These corporations, with their financial strength and distribution capabilities, can complete the value chain and accelerate time-to-market. While such processes offer financial returns and new growth prospects, they also require careful management of the IOR to preserve the specialized competencies and agile decision-making processes that often characterize smaller biotech firms. M&A is also the most widespread exit strategy, enabling quick monetization of developed knowledge while fueling a virtuous cycle of reinvestment and entrepreneurial renewal. In this way, the innovation ecosystem is strengthened, capital and expertise circulate, new ideas emerge, and the sector's overall competitiveness is enhanced.

In conclusion, strategic IORs and M&A transactions together outline a developmental trajectory for the biotech sector that leverages its inherently collaborative nature. When well-managed, these partnerships offer multiple pathways for value creation, balancing innovation, competitiveness, and integration in an increasingly globalized and dynamic marketplace (Doz, Santos & Williamson, 2001).

CHAPTER 3

Managing Innovation: Business Models and Strategic Configurations in Biotech Firms

Abstract: This chapter examines the strategic management of innovation in biotechnology firms, focusing on how scientific knowledge is translated into viable business models and technological opportunities. In highly knowledge-intensive environments characterized by scientific uncertainty and long development cycles, firms must design organizational configurations that integrate research activities, intellectual property management, and collaborative networks. The chapter analyzes the main business model configurations observed in the biotechnology sector, including dedicated biotech firms, integrated biotech firms, fully integrated firms, and hybrid models such as platform-based and service-oriented approaches. Through comparative observations across Italy, Spain, the United Kingdom, and South Korea, the analysis highlights how institutional environments, innovation policies, and scientific clusters shape firms' strategic choices and innovation trajectories. Particular attention is devoted to the role of collaborative ecosystems, open innovation practices, and emerging digital technologies in supporting the transformation of scientific discoveries into scalable solutions. The chapter demonstrates that strategic innovation in biotechnology requires aligning scientific capabilities, organizational structures, and innovation networks to create sustainable competitive advantage.

Keywords: AI, Biotech business models, Innovation management, Innovation ecosystems, Knowledge-intensive firms, Strategic innovation.

INTRODUCTION

The preceding chapters have highlighted how the biotech sector is characterized by a profound interdependence between science, technology, market dynamics, and regulatory frameworks, making a dynamic strategic approach and the ability to establish collaborative networks essential. In more detail, Chapter 1 has shown how the external context profoundly influences the strategic decisions of European biotech firms, while Chapter 2 has illustrated how IORs represent key strategic alternatives to respond to the needs of a rapidly evolving sector, in which the search for new therapeutic, industrial, or environmental solutions necessitates the sharing of expertise, knowledge, costs, and risks.

Paola Olimpia Achard

Building on these considerations, this chapter focuses on the strategic management of innovation within biotech firms. In knowledge-intensive industries such as biotechnology, firms do not merely exploit scientific discoveries; rather, they must integrate them into coherent business models that transform research outcomes into valuable products, services, or technological platforms. The ability to design and manage appropriate innovation strategies, therefore, represents a critical success factor for firms operating in highly uncertain and regulated environments.

Unlike many traditional industries, where barriers to entry are mainly economic or technological, biotechnology is characterized by a unique combination of scientific complexity, regulatory constraints, and substantial investments in research and development. Firms must therefore adopt flexible organizational configurations and strategic approaches capable of supporting long development cycles and managing high levels of uncertainty.

Within this context, the chapter analyzes the main business models adopted by firms operating in the biotech sector and examines how they organize research activities, manage intellectual property, and develop collaborative networks with universities, research institutions, and industrial partners. Attention is devoted to the strategic configurations through which biotech firms structure their innovation processes and position themselves within broader scientific and technological ecosystems (Onetti & Zucchella, 2014; Eudaric & Pellegrin, 2026).

Through analysis of different national contexts, the chapter highlights how innovation pathways may differ across institutional environments while converging on a common objective: maximizing the value generated by scientific knowledge and transforming it into high-impact solutions for the economy and society. In this perspective, strategic innovation emerges as a key mechanism through which biotech firms translate scientific capabilities into competitive advantage.

BUSINESS MODELS FOR INNOVATION MANAGEMENT

The strategic management of innovation in biotech firms involves a continuous, complex process of translating scientific outcomes into products and/or services that can be deployed across multiple subsectors, including healthcare, environmental applications, agriculture, and industry. This process must take place within the confines of regulatory frameworks that are often highly stringent and constantly evolving. In such a complex environment, the business model assumes a central role. It defines how the firm creates, delivers, and captures value from knowledge, whether developed internally or acquired through IORs (Pisano, 2006; Pires & Ferreira, 2025; Sorrentino & Garraffo, 2012).

The distinctive strategic features of the biotech sector, such as intensive capital requirements, the protracted duration of R&D cycles, and the high probability of project failure, generate corporate behaviors and strategic choices that differ markedly from those observed in more traditional sectors, such as manufacturing or services. Therefore, it is important to explore the fundamental components that shape the business models of biotech firms, analyzing how firms strategically integrate scientific research, partnership configurations, and the valorization of IP to sustain innovation trajectories and build competitive advantage (Bianchi *et al.*, 2011; Bigliardi, Nosella & Verbano, 2005).

The Architecture of the Business Model in Biotech Firms

The business model defines how a firm creates, delivers, and captures value. In concrete terms, it describes how the firm generates economic, social, and environmental value by offering specific products or services to targeted customer segments, while optimally organizing the resources and activities required to do so. A clearly defined business model supports strategic decision-making, facilitates differentiation from competitors, and enables rapid adaptation to changes in the competitive environment (Niosi & McKelvey, 2018; Osterwalder & Pigneur, 2010; Shafer, Smith & Linder, 2005; Teece, 2018).

Table 5. Canvas business model articulation (own elaboration).

-	Who/What are They?	Why are Important
Key partnerships	The network of suppliers, distributors, and external partners that support the firm through various IORs.	They make it possible to acquire skills, resources, or channels that the firm does not possess internally, reducing costs and risks while accelerating innovation.
Key activities	The key activities the firm must carry out to make the business model work.	They allow the firm to focus on activities that generate real value for the customer and differentiate it from the competition.
Value propositions	The set of benefits and solutions that the firm offers to satisfy customer needs or solve their problems.	They represent the main reason why customers choose one offering over another; they clarify the very purpose of the firm's existence.
Customer relationships	The type of relationship established with each customer segment.	Defining how to interact with customers influences loyalty, satisfaction, and ultimately the firm's sales and reputation.
Customer segments	Distinct groups of individuals, firms, or institutions to which the firm directs its offering.	Precisely defining customer segments means focusing marketing efforts on the real needs of those who will benefit from the products or services.
Key resources	The key assets the company must own or acquire to create and deliver the value proposition.	Without the right resources it is impossible to implement the desired business model.

(Table 5) cont.....

-	Who/What are They?	Why are Important
Channels	The ways in which the firm reaches its customer segments and delivers the value proposition to them.	They allow the offering to be known, enable its purchase, and ensure effective delivery of products or services.
Cost structure	All the expenses required to start up and operate the business model.	Understanding the cost structure helps assess the firm's profitability and establish appropriate pricing strategies.
Revenue streams	They represent the way the firm generates revenue from each customer segment.	They identify sources of revenue and allow understanding which offerings and customer segments are the most profitable or strategic.

The Business Model Canvas developed by Osterwalder & Pigneur (2010), provides a clear and concise overview of how a firm creates and delivers value. The BMC is a visual tool that enables the description and analysis of a business model through nine fundamental building blocks (Table **5**). When analyzing the business model in the biotech sector, it is necessary to consider several defining elements: focus on research; valorization of IP; value system and network; cost structure and revenue streams; and centrality for risk management. These elements are analyzed in the following sections.

FOCUS ON RESEARCH

Most biotech firms originate as university spin-offs or research lab initiatives, with the primary aim of validating a scientific discovery and transforming it into a marketable product or service. This pronounced orientation towards R&D is reflected in a corporate culture that emphasizes ongoing scientific development and the pursuit of highly specialized talent, such as biologists, chemists, bioinformaticians, and biomedical engineers. Frequently, firms concentrate their efforts on a single therapeutic area (in the case of red biotechnology) or on a specific technology (for example, gene editing), seeking to establish a long-term competitive advantage and secure faster, more defensible IP positions.

Valorization of Intellectual Property

Intangible assets, such as patents, know-how, trademarks, and licenses, constitute the real engine of growth for many firms in the sector. Unlike traditional industrial firms, biotech firms are often able to generate value by developing a single molecule or platform that may subsequently be licensed to larger operators. Legal protection and the strategic management of IP rights become critical activities. Firms must carefully assess where to file patents, how to structure licensing agreements, and how to safeguard themselves from potential imitation (Grebe & Jarchow, 2025).

Value System and Network: Partnerships and Collaborative Relationships

Biotech firms seldom operate in isolation. On the contrary, they are embedded within an ecosystem that includes universities, research centers, financial institutions, large multinational pharmaceutical firms (as well as firms from adjacent sectors such as healthcare), incubators, and governmental agencies. IORs, as discussed in Chapter 2, play a fundamental role in mitigating or overcoming barriers linked to the high costs of R&D, limited access to complementary scientific and managerial expertise, and the need for advanced research infrastructure. These partnerships are essential for enhancing the firm's capacity to innovate and navigate the sector's structural complexity.

Cost Structure and Revenue Streams

In biotechnology business models, the cost structure is typically characterized by a high incidence of research and regulatory expenditures, such as clinical trials, approvals, and certifications, compared to the actual costs of production or service delivery. Revenue streams may stem from the direct sale of final products (including pharmaceuticals, diagnostic tests, industrial enzymes, and related outputs), as well as from licensing patents or from third-party development and analysis services, particularly for firms that own technological platforms applicable across multiple sectors. Furthermore, it is important to account for the role of public and private funding, such as grants and venture capital, which sustain the early stages of a firm's development and often determine its capacity to survive, given that returns on investment are typically deferred over a multi-year horizon.

Centrality of Risk Management

The development cycle of a biotechnology product or service is characterized by high uncertainty. Scientific risk arises from the possibility that the research hypothesis may not lead to tangible results. Regulatory risk stems from the potential for delays or rejections by the competent authorities. Market risk, in turn, may stem from changes in competitive dynamics, healthcare reimbursement policies, or patient and other end-user acceptance levels.

An effective business model must incorporate rigorous risk management methodologies, including diversification strategies, such as pursuing multiple research lines in parallel, as well as risk mitigation mechanisms, for example, by engaging in partnerships with larger firms or adopting milestone-based payment structures tied to the achievement of intermediate results (Folta, 1998).

Typical Configurations and Evolutionary Perspectives of Business Models

Within the biotech sector, several recurrent business model configurations can be identified, generally labeled Dedicated Biotech Firm (DBF), Innovative Biotech Firm (IBF), and Fully Integrated Firm (FIF). These configurations, however, are inherently dynamic and subject to continuous evolution, influenced by the firm's maturity stage and the opportunities emerging from the broader macro-environment (Quintana-Garcia & Benavides-Velasco, 2004). For each of them, it is possible to identify specific characteristics, peculiar key elements, and specific challenges and advantages.

Firms adopting the DBF model focus predominantly on R&D in the biotechnology domain, often on a specific therapeutic area or technology (Shimasaki, 2008, 2014). This approach is typical of university spin-offs or research laboratory ventures characterized by high scientific specialization. Among the key elements, it can be mentioned that, for firms adopting the DBF model, funding is generally secured through venture capital, public grants, or co-development partnerships with pharmaceutical firms. For these firms, the organizational culture emphasizes continuous innovation, backed by substantial investments in human resources, particularly in researchers and highly specialized scientific profiles. In terms of challenges and advantages, it is worth highlighting that while these firms tend to be relatively lean in structure and enjoy considerable strategic flexibility, they also face significant risk exposure. The failure of a single project can threaten the firm's very survival. IP represents the core value driver, with licensing of molecules, analytical methods, or technological platforms constituting a critical revenue source (Bigliardi *et al.*, 2005; Quintana-Garcia & Benavides-Velasco, 2004; Sorrentino & Garraffo, 2012).

Firms adopting the IBF model, in turn, integrate biotechnological expertise into pre-existing products or processes, where biotechnology is not the sole focus of the value proposition. IBFs are frequently found in sectors such as healthcare, agri-food, the chemical industry, energy, or environmental services. Among the key elements of IBFs is certainly the fact that these firms possess hybrid knowledge bases, combining biotechnology with other disciplinary fields, leveraging science to enhance the efficiency or quality of existing products and thereby broadening the portfolio of marketable solutions. Open innovation collaborations with public or private research institutions are common for firms adopting the IBF model, facilitating knowledge acquisition and accelerating development cycles (Bianchi *et al.*, 2011). As far as challenges and advantages are concerned, IBFs exhibit greater risk diversification than DBFs, as their revenue streams are typically drawn from multiple business lines rather than hinging on a single experimental drug or technology. However, the biotechnology component may constitute only a relatively minor share of overall costs, which can constrain substantial R&D investments unless supported by external partners or public incentives.

Firms adopting the FIF model maintain control over the entire value chain, encompassing research, production, and commercialization of biotechnology products or services. This approach demands extensive managerial capabilities and significant financial resources to concurrently manage R&D activities, production operations, and strategic collaboration networks (Pisano, 2006; Skvarka & Farkas, 2013). Key elements of FIFs include full oversight across all development phases, which reduces reliance on external partners and enhances the firm's ability to manage time-to-market effectively. It also enables the capture of the full economic benefits of innovation without sharing exploitation rights with third parties, except in specific strategic alliances. Finally, in terms of challenges and advantages, it should be noted that the initial investment required for firms adopting this model is substantial, and failure to obtain regulatory approval or commercial success for a product can result in significant financial losses for the entire firm. This model is generally characteristic of mature biotech firms capable of sustaining the high costs associated with R&D, clinical trials, and large-scale production and service delivery.

Beyond these three primary business models, additional configurations can be distinguished, such as the Pure R&D model, which is comparable to an early-stage DBF and relies heavily on public funding and private equity, focusing primarily on scientific discoveries intended for transfer to industrial partners. Another model is the so-called platform model, which shares characteristics with DBFs (high-tech focus) and IBFs (application flexibility). Its value is anchored in core technologies that can be applied across multiple domains, such as oncology, agriculture, and diagnostics. Finally, there is the service provider model, common among biotech firms functioning as Contract Research Organizations (CROs) or Contract Manufacturing Organizations (CMOs). According to this model, firms complete the supply chain by offering third-party production, testing, or production services.

Generally speaking, the business model of biotech firms typically revolves around four fundamental pillars: i) research and IP management, which steer investment priorities and strategic decisions; ii) partnerships, collaborative networks, and open innovation, which are essential to mitigate the high costs and complexity of scientific research; iii) a cost structure dominated by experimental activities and regulatory compliance, often associated with long time-to-market; iv) strategic risk management, necessitated by the inherent uncertainties of scientific outcomes and market dynamics (Esfandyarpour *et al.*, 2024; Teece, 2018). Firms may adopt these pillars in configurations that are more focused (DBFs), technologically hybridized (IBFs), or vertically integrated (FIFs). Additionally, transversal approaches, such as Pure R&D, Platform-Based models, and Third-Party service provision, highlight specific supply chain activities. Ultimately, the choice of a particular business model depends on various factors including the firm's maturity, level of scientific specialization, availability of financial resources, and the characteristics of the scientific clusters and ecosystems within which the firm operates (Chiaroni, Chiesa, & Frattini, 2008; Powell, 1996; Sobrero & Roberts, 2002; Wilson & York, 2023).

The Role of Policy and Scientific Clusters

In shaping the business models of biotech firms, the national system and broader macro-environment in which they operate exert a decisive influence. Elements such as the availability of public funding, the strength of the academic research ecosystem, the presence of incubators and technology parks, capital market regulation, and the ease of establishing connections with international or global partners can significantly enable, or, conversely, hinder, the development of innovative business models. To gain a greater understanding of these dynamics, it is interesting to explore four national contexts: Italy, Spain, the UK, and South Korea, highlighting the principal mechanisms through which biotech firms manage innovation (Kang & Park, 2012).

Focus on Business Models in Italy

In Italy, a significant proportion of biotech firms emerge as university spin-offs or are founded by researchers aiming to commercialize scientific discoveries. These firms are frequently built around a single innovative project and tend to adopt either a Pure R&D model or operate as Third-Party service providers, establishing partnerships with large pharmaceutical firms or other global players. It follows that SMEs and micro-firms are prevalent among Italian biotech firms. Certain regions, such as Lombardy, Piedmont, and Tuscany, offer more mature and integrated innovation ecosystems, where universities, innovation hubs, and firms collaborate in a coordinated fashion. Therefore, regional clusters and districts assume a very relevant role. These regional clusters foster the development of supply chains that facilitate the sharing of know-how, laboratory infrastructure, and technology transfer services (Biocat, 2023; Vurro *et al.*, 2024). Finally, in Italy, the role of collaborative strategies proves to be extremely important for biotech firms. Indeed, given the limited financial resources of smaller firms, partnerships with big pharma, the formation of joint ventures, and participation in consortia, particularly to access European funding instruments (*e.g.*, Horizon Europe, mission-driven research calls), become critical strategic levers. In return for licensing rights or equity stakes, SMEs gain access to the capital necessary to carry out clinical trials and move forward in product or service development.

Focus on Business Models in Spain

In recent years, Spain has experienced a sharp increase in the number of biotech start-ups. Many of these firms focus on specialized niches (*e.g.*, cell therapies, advanced diagnostics) and aim to license or sell their technologies to larger industry players once scientific proof of concept is achieved (Biocat, 2023). The proximity of academic institutions (especially in Barcelona, Madrid, and Valencia) to incubators has created fertile ground for spin-offs adopting either Platform-Based models or Pure R&D approaches. Public funding at both the regional and national levels, combined with European funding mechanisms, plays a pivotal role in supporting early-stage ventures. For Spanish biotech firms, internationalization has become a strategic imperative. Due to the relatively small domestic market, many Spanish biotech firms adopt an international outlook from the outset, seeking partnerships abroad or targeting exports to regions with more favorable regulatory conditions for specific applications, such as Latin America or parts of Asia.

Focus on Business Models in the UK

The UK boasts a long-standing tradition of excellence in scientific research, notably at institutions such as Oxford, Cambridge, Imperial College, and UCL, and a highly developed financial system that is well-positioned to channel substantial venture capital into high-potential biotech firms (Finegold & Frenkel, 2006; Office for Life Sciences, 2017; PricewaterhouseCoopers LLP, 2025; Wilson & York, 2023). Therefore, the UK can be considered a Global Life Sciences Hub. British biotech firms usually adopt a hybrid business model (IBFs). Many start-ups scale through venture capital funding, develop breakthrough technologies, and subsequently choose between vertical integration or out-licensing their IP to global pharmaceutical firms. In several instances, big pharma based in the UK engages directly in technology scouting and acquisition of the most promising start-ups (Trincado-Munoz *et al.*, 2022). To conclude, with the focus on business models in the UK, it should be noted that the country has a pro-innovation fiscal policy. R&D tax credits and schemes such as the Patent Box incentivize the creation of innovative firms and encourage experimentation with new business models. As a result, firms are often able to adopt a global market orientation from the earliest stages of their development.

Focus on Business Models in South Korea

South Korea has articulated a clear, long-term vision for the development of its biotech sector, supported by multi-year plans and substantial investments in research infrastructure and the development of specialized human resources. Major conglomerates such as Samsung and LG have established dedicated biotechnology divisions, often adopting an integrated model in which R&D, production, and distribution are managed internally. At the same time, a vibrant ecosystem of innovative SMEs has emerged, many of which follow either a Pure R&D or a Platform-Based model and collaborate closely with these industrial giants. A distinctive feature of the South Korean biotechnology landscape is the convergence of biotechnology and information technology, particularly in big data and AI. This integration has given rise to firms that combine biological expertise with digital capabilities, offering predictive diagnostics services and highly automated screening platforms (Arden *et al.*, 2021; Etit *et al.*, 2024).

Key Challenges and Future Perspectives

The analysis of business models for innovation management within the biotech sector reveals several overarching challenges, each of which is explored in depth below (Helfat & Martin, 2015).

Balancing Specialization with Diversification

Firms that are highly specialized can have a niche market and gain a competitive advantage in that space. However, this focus also exposes them to significant risks, particularly related to technological shifts or the failure of key projects. Diversification, such as developing multiple research lines and branching into different business areas, can mitigate some of these risks by spreading them across a broader portfolio. However, diversification comes with its own set of challenges, including higher coordination and management costs.

Prolonged Development Timelines and Regulatory Uncertainty

The biotechnology drug development process is notoriously long and costly, often exceeding 10 years and requiring hundreds of millions, if not billions, of euros in investment. Given this extended timeline, firms must structure their business models to be financially sustainable over the long term. This can be achieved by securing flexible funding sources and generating interim revenue streams through licensing agreements, contract services, or collaborations with other research entities. Moreover, the complexity and unpredictability of regulatory environments, particularly in the pharmaceutical and healthcare sector, add another layer of uncertainty. Regulatory frameworks can change unexpectedly, leading to potential delays, additional compliance costs, or the need for further adjustments in clinical trials and approval processes. Consequently, biotech firms must continually innovate not only in scientific development but also in adapting to shifting regulatory landscapes (DiMasi, Grabowski, & Hansen 2016).

Global Competition and the Need for International Expansion

Biotechnology competition is no longer confined to local or national markets. Global powerhouses, particularly in the USA and China, exert significant pressure on international markets, forcing European and South Korean firms to constantly raise the bar on research excellence and product quality. Therefore, many biotech firms find that achieving meaningful scale requires internationalization. This process often involves navigating complex regulatory environments across different regions and securing cross-border partnerships with research institutions, multinational corporations, and healthcare providers. As a result, firms must build strong capabilities in international business management, including global marketing strategies and regulatory affairs, to compete effectively on the world stage (Pisano, 2006; Powell, 1996).

Artificial Intelligence and Ecosystem-Based Innovation in the Strategic Transformation of Biotech Firms

Recent developments underscore the growing importance of open innovation, a model where businesses, research institutions, and even public organizations share knowledge, data, and technologies in pre-competitive phases (Bruneo *et al.*, 2024; Chiaroni, Chiesa & Frattini, 2008; Junkunc, 2007). This collaborative approach accelerates the discovery of novel solutions by reducing duplication of effort and enabling more rapid progress. AI and machine learning are increasingly transforming drug discovery and biomedical research processes by enabling the analysis of large-scale biological datasets (Ashley, 2016; Vamathevan *et al.*, 2019; Chen *et al.*, 2018). Indeed, they are dramatically reshaping R&D paradigms within the biotech sector (King, 2025; Mak & Pichika, 2019; Vamathevan *et al.*, 2019). The ability to process vast amounts of genomic, phenotypic, and clinical data is transforming drug discovery and enabling new approaches to precision medicine and biomedical research (Ashley, 2016; Topol, 2019). The ability to process vast amounts of genomic, phenotypic, and clinical data is transforming drug discovery, enabling faster, more accurate predictions of treatment efficacy. This section examines how artificial intelligence and ecosystem-based innovation jointly reshape business models, organizational configurations, and capability development in biotech firms.

The integration of AI could even disrupt traditional phases of drug screening and testing, enabling firms to leverage data-driven insights for more effective decision-making. As a result, biotech firms that have historically focused on pure R&D may evolve into data science solution providers, offering advanced analytics and predictive modeling capabilities. In this new landscape, AI-driven platforms could supplement or even replace conventional methods in drug screening, clinical trials, and patient monitoring.

The integration of AI into biotechnology innovation processes can be interpreted not only as a technological evolution but also as a broader transformation of firms' strategic architecture. AI-driven innovation influences four interconnected dimensions of biotech firms: the nature of scientific discovery processes, the configuration of business models, the development of organizational capabilities, and the evolution of professional roles within firms. Indeed, AI is transforming the mechanisms of scientific discovery. The traditional biotechnology innovation process, largely based on laboratory experimentation and sequential validation, is increasingly complemented by computational approaches that analyze vast volumes of biological and clinical data. Machine learning models allow researchers to identify patterns, generate predictive insights, and simulate molecular interactions, thereby accelerating the identification of promising research trajectories. Therefore, scientific discovery in biotechnology is increasingly shifting toward hybrid research models that integrate AI-based computational prediction with experimental validation in laboratory environments (Schneider *et al.*, 2020; Chen *et al.*, 2018).

These technological transformations are influencing the design and evolution of biotech firms' business models. Traditionally, value creation in the biotech sector has been closely associated with the discovery and development of specific molecules, therapeutic compounds, or specialized biological applications. While these product-based innovation trajectories remain central to many biotech firms, the integration of AI and data-driven research infrastructures is progressively expanding the range of strategic options available for value creation. Biotech firms are increasingly able to generate value not only through the commercialization of individual products but also through the development and management of technological platforms that process biological and clinical data. These platforms integrate biological knowledge, computational modelling, and large-scale data analytics to support multiple research activities simultaneously. Rather than focusing exclusively on a single research project or therapeutic target, platform-based biotech firms can leverage their technological infrastructures across a variety of scientific applications, including drug discovery, biomarker identification, diagnostics, and personalized medicine.

The strategic relevance of these platforms lies in their scalability. Once developed, data-driven technological infrastructures can be applied across multiple research contexts at relatively low marginal cost. This scalability enables biotech firms to diversify their innovation pipelines while maintaining a coherent technological core. For instance, a computational platform designed to analyze genomic datasets for oncology research may also be adapted to support investigations in rare diseases, immunology, or metabolic disorders. In this way, the technological infrastructure becomes a central asset around which the firm's business model is organized.

Moreover, AI-enabled business models enable biotech firms to develop new forms of value capture beyond traditional product commercialization. Firms may generate revenue through licensing agreements, collaborative research partnerships, data-driven services, or the provision of analytical platforms to external partners. In such configurations, biotech firms operate not only as developers of biological products but also as providers of technological capabilities that support innovation processes across the broader life sciences ecosystem.

This evolution also alters the strategic positioning of biotech firms within innovation networks. Firms that control advanced data infrastructures and analytical platforms can occupy central positions within collaborative ecosystems, acting as technological intermediaries that connect scientific knowledge, clinical evidence, and industrial development processes. Consequently, the design of business models in AI-enabled biotech firms increasingly depends on the ability to combine scientific discovery, digital infrastructures, and collaborative innovation strategies within a coherent strategic architecture (Teece, 2018; Pisano, 2006).

The diffusion of AI requires biotech firms to develop new organizational capabilities. The integration of AI into biotechnology innovation processes involves combining heterogeneous forms of expertise, infrastructures, and knowledge bases that traditionally belonged to separate domains. As a result, biotech firms must progressively evolve from purely science-driven organizations toward more complex organizational systems capable of integrating biological research with digital technologies and advanced data analytics. At the core of this transformation lies the need to develop capabilities that enable firms to manage interdisciplinary knowledge. Scientific expertise in areas such as molecular biology, genetics, pharmacology, and biochemistry must increasingly interact with competencies in data science, machine learning, computational modelling, and digital infrastructure management. This integration requires biotech firms to develop coordination mechanisms that facilitate communication and collaboration between different professional communities whose epistemic cultures and research practices may differ significantly. In addition, biotech firms must strengthen their capabilities in managing digital infrastructures and data governance systems. The effective use of AI depends on the availability of large, high-quality datasets and the capacity to store, process, and analyze them in secure, reliable environments. Consequently, firms must invest in data architectures that ensure interoperability among diverse data sources, including genomic databases, clinical trial datasets, and real-world patient information. At the same time, firms must ensure compliance with evolving regulatory frameworks related to data protection, patient privacy, and ethical standards in biomedical research.

From a strategic management perspective, these requirements call for the development of dynamic capabilities that enable biotech firms to continuously adapt their innovation processes. Firms must be able to integrate new technological tools, reconfigure research infrastructures, and reorganize collaborative relationships in response to scientific and regulatory changes. The ability to orchestrate complex combinations of scientific knowledge, technological resources, and external partnerships becomes a critical factor in sustaining innovation performance over time (see chapter 2).

Ultimately, AI-driven innovation challenges traditional organizational models in biotechnology. Rather than relying on linear research processes organized around specialized laboratory activities, biotech firms increasingly operate through distributed innovation systems where experimentation, data analysis, and computational modelling interact continuously (Ashley, 2020; Topol, 2019). Firms that successfully develop the organizational capabilities required to manage these complex innovation processes are more likely to maintain strategic flexibility and to respond effectively to the rapidly evolving dynamics of the biotechnology sector (see chapter 1). These transformations are also reshaping the composition of human capital within biotech firms. Historically, biotech firms have relied primarily on highly specialized scientific professionals such as molecular biologists, chemists, pharmacologists, and biomedical engineers. These profiles remain fundamental to the development of new therapeutic and technological solutions. However, the growing importance of AI and data-driven research is expanding the range of competencies required within biotech firms.

Biotech firms increasingly require hybrid professional profiles capable of operating at the intersection of biotechnology and data science. Bioinformaticians, computational biologists, data scientists, and machine learning specialists are becoming integral members of research teams, contributing to the analysis and interpretation of large-scale biological datasets. Their role is not limited to supporting computational tasks; rather, these professionals actively shape research strategies by identifying patterns in complex datasets and generating predictive insights that guide experimental design. The presence of these hybrid competencies is transforming the internal organization of research activities within biotech firms. Innovation increasingly emerges from collaborative interactions between laboratory scientists and computational specialists. For example, experimental researchers may generate biological data through laboratory experiments, while data scientists develop analytical models to identify correlations, predict molecular interactions, or optimize clinical trial design. This iterative interaction between experimentation and computation accelerates innovation cycles and improves the efficiency of research processes. At the same time, the expansion of data-driven innovation is creating demand for additional professional roles related to data management, digital infrastructure, and regulatory oversight. Specialists in data governance, data engineering, and digital health compliance are becoming increasingly relevant in ensuring that data collection, storage, and analysis processes comply with regulatory standards and ethical requirements. These roles are particularly important in contexts involving sensitive clinical data or patient-related information.

For biotech firms, managing this evolving landscape of competencies represents a significant strategic challenge. Firms must develop recruitment strategies, training programs, and organizational cultures that can integrate professionals with diverse disciplinary backgrounds. Encouraging collaboration among scientists, engineers, and data specialists is essential to exploit the opportunities offered by AI and data-driven research fully. Biotech firms that successfully attract and integrate these emerging professional profiles are better positioned to build resilient innovation capabilities and sustain competitive advantage in increasingly knowledge-intensive, technologically complex environments. Consequently, biotech firms must develop organizational environments that foster collaboration among diverse professional communities and facilitate knowledge exchange across disciplinary boundaries.

These dimensions illustrate how AI is progressively redefining the strategic foundations of biotechnology firms. Rather than being a simple technological tool, AI operates as a catalyst for broader transformations that affect how firms generate knowledge, design business models, organize internal capabilities, and structure their workforce. These transformations are particularly visible in several emerging configurations of AI-enabled biotech firms. While the boundaries between them are often fluid, three broad strategic patterns can be observed: AI-enabled discovery firms, platform-based biotech firms, and data-driven ecosystem firms. Table **6** summarizes the main configurations through which AI is transforming biotech firms: discovery-oriented, platform-based, and data-driven ecosystem firms.

Table 6. AI-Enabled Configurations of Biotech Firms (own elaboration, based on Mak & Pichika, 2019; Vamathevan *et al.*, 2019; Teece, 2018; Chiaroni, Chiesa & Frattini, 2008; Pisano, 2006; Powell *et al.*, 1996).

Configuration of Biotech Firms	Strategic Focus	Illustrative Examples
AI-Enabled Discovery Biotech Firms	Artificial intelligence accelerates scientific discovery and drug identification.	Exscientia; Insilico Medicine
Platform-Based Biotech Firms	AI platforms support multiple research pipelines and scalable innovation.	Recursion Pharmaceuticals; BioNTech
Data-Driven Ecosystem Biotech Firms	Integration and orchestration of large clinical and genomic data ecosystems.	Tempus; Owkin

The strategic role of AI is particularly evident in a growing group of biotech firms that primarily use it to accelerate scientific discovery (Zhavoronkov *et al.*, 2019). These organizations typically integrate machine learning algorithms into traditional drug discovery pipelines to identify therapeutic targets, screen molecular compounds, and optimize experimental design. In these cases, AI does not fundamentally alter the product-oriented nature of the business model but significantly improves the efficiency and speed of research and development activities.

An illustrative example is Exscientia, a biotechnology firm founded in the United Kingdom as a spin-off from the University of Dundee. The firm operates in AI-driven drug discovery, developing computational platforms that support the design of small-molecule drugs using machine learning and advanced molecular modelling. Exscientia has developed multiple drug candidates designed using AI. The firm employs several hundred professionals and has established partnerships with large pharmaceutical companies such as Sanofi and Bristol Myers Squibb, demonstrating how AI-enabled discovery models can complement traditional pharmaceutical development pipelines. Another widely cited example is Insilico Medicine, an international biotech firm specializing in generative AI for drug discovery. The firm develops deep learning models capable of identifying novel molecular structures and predicting biological activity across multiple therapeutic domains. Through its AI-driven research platforms, Insilico Medicine has generated several drug candidates for diseases such as fibrosis and oncology. With operations spanning multiple research hubs and a rapidly growing workforce of data scientists and biomedical researchers, the firm exemplifies how AI can significantly shorten the time from target identification to preclinical development.

The evolution toward platform-oriented business models is another important consequence of AI integration within biotech firms. In these configurations, firms develop technological infrastructures that combine biological data, machine learning algorithms, and computational modelling tools to support multiple research applications simultaneously. Rather than focusing exclusively on a single therapeutic product, these biotech firms build scalable innovation platforms that generate insights across multiple therapeutic and research domains.

A prominent example is Recursion Pharmaceuticals, a biotech firm established in the United States that has developed a large-scale machine learning platform integrating biological imaging, automation, and AI. The firm analyzes millions of cellular images to identify biological patterns that may support drug discovery across multiple disease areas. Recursion employs hundreds of scientists, engineers, and computational specialists and has established partnerships with several global pharmaceutical companies. Its platform-based model illustrates how technological infrastructures can become the central strategic asset around which the firm's innovation activities are organized.

A European example of this platform-based configuration is BioNTech, a German biotechnology firm known internationally for developing mRNA-based technologies. While widely recognized for its COVID-19 vaccine developed in collaboration with Pfizer, BioNTech's core innovation strategy is based on computational platforms that integrate genomics, immunology, and machine learning to identify tumor-specific neoantigens and support the development of personalized cancer immunotherapies. The firm employs several thousand professionals across its research and manufacturing facilities and generates multi-billion-euro annual revenues, illustrating how AI-enabled platform infrastructures can support large-scale innovation pipelines in advanced biotechnology domains.

A third configuration emerging from the integration of AI within biotechnology is represented by biotech firms that operate as central nodes within data-driven innovation ecosystems. These firms derive strategic advantage not only from proprietary technologies but also from their capacity to integrate and analyze large-scale clinical, genomic, and biomedical datasets generated across healthcare systems.

An illustrative example is Tempus, a biotechnology and technology firm specializing in precision medicine and data-driven oncology research. Tempus collects and analyzes large volumes of clinical and genomic data obtained from hospitals and research institutions, applying AI to identify patterns that support diagnostic and therapeutic decision-making. The firm collaborates with healthcare providers and pharmaceutical firms and has built one of the largest clinical-genomic datasets in oncology, employing thousands of professionals across data science, medical research, and digital infrastructure management.

Another relevant example is Owkin, a European biotechnology firm headquartered in France that develops AI models for biomedical research through collaborations with hospitals and pharmaceutical companies. Owkin uses advanced machine learning techniques, including federated learning, to analyze sensitive clinical datasets while preserving patient privacy. The firm operates within a broad network of medical institutions and research partners, demonstrating how biotech firms can position themselves as orchestrators of complex data ecosystems that connect healthcare providers, researchers, and pharmaceutical developers. Ultimately, the strategic relevance of AI lies not only in its technological potential but in how biotech firms integrate it into their business models, organizational capabilities, and innovation ecosystems.

CONCLUDING REMARKS

The analysis developed in this chapter highlights how strategic innovation management is a central element in defining the competitive positioning of biotech firms. In knowledge-intensive industries characterized by high levels of uncertainty, long development cycles, and strong regulatory constraints, firms must design business models capable of transforming scientific discoveries into viable technological and market opportunities. The adoption of diversified business models - ranging from Pure R&D approaches and platform-based models to more integrated configurations that combine research, development, and commercialization - demonstrates that defining an appropriate strategic architecture is essential to cope with the inherent complexity of the biotech sector. Each configuration reflects different combinations of scientific specialization, financial resources, and organizational capabilities, as well as different approaches to collaboration with universities, research centers, and industrial partners.

Across different institutional contexts, biotech firms operate within innovation ecosystems shaped by national policies, scientific infrastructures, and access to financial capital. These ecosystems influence firms' strategic choices, including the selection of innovation pathways, the formation of collaborative networks, and the development of technological platforms that support multiple applications.

Ultimately, the chapter shows that strategic innovation in the biotech sector cannot be reduced to the simple exploitation of scientific knowledge. Rather, it requires the ability to structure coherent business models, mobilize interdisciplinary competencies, and position the firm within complex scientific and technological networks. When effectively governed, these elements enable biotech firms to translate scientific capabilities into competitive advantage and to contribute to the broader process of knowledge-driven economic development.

CHAPTER 4

Value-Generating Activities and Strategic Resources in Biotech Firms

Abstract: This chapter analyzes the internal processes through which biotechnology firms generate and organize value along their innovation and production activities. Using the value chain framework as the main analytical lens, the chapter examines how primary and support activities interact to transform scientific discoveries into marketable products and services. Attention is devoted to the role of organizational resources and competencies in sustaining long-term competitive advantage. In biotechnology, tangible resources such as laboratories and research infrastructure interact closely with intangible assets, including scientific knowledge, technological platforms, intellectual capital, and relational networks. The chapter highlights how integrating these elements enables firms to manage complex innovation processes, coordinate regulatory and technological requirements, and sustain the long development cycles typical of the sector. By examining the interdependence between value-generating activities and strategic resources, the chapter demonstrates that competitive advantage in biotechnology depends not only on scientific breakthroughs but also on the organizational capacity to coordinate resources, competencies, and operational processes in highly uncertain environments.

Keywords: Core competencies, Organizational capabilities, Resource-based view, Dtrategic resources, Value chain.

INTRODUCTION

While the previous chapter has examined the strategic configurations through which biotech firms manage innovation and design their business models, the present chapter shifts the focus to the internal mechanisms through which scientific knowledge is transformed into economic and organizational value. In highly knowledge-intensive sectors such as biotechnology, innovation outcomes depend not only on the quality of research activities but also on the effective coordination of the multiple activities involved in development, production, and commercialization processes.

To analyze these dynamics, the chapter adopts the value chain framework originally proposed by Porter (1985), which enables the systematic examination of the set of activities through which firms create value for their stakeholders.

Paola Olimpia Achard

Within biotech firms, value-generating activities span the management of research inputs and laboratory operations, regulatory interactions, production processes, and market access strategies. Each of these stages requires integrating specialized competencies, technological infrastructures, and organizational routines that support long, complex development cycles.

Attention is devoted to the role of strategic resources and organizational competencies in sustaining competitive advantage. In biotechnology, tangible assets such as laboratories, research infrastructures, and production facilities interact with intangible resources including scientific know-how, intellectual capital, technological platforms, and relational networks. The effective integration of these resources enables firms to coordinate complex innovation processes and to manage the high levels of uncertainty that characterize the sector.

By examining both primary and support activities, the chapter highlights how biotech firms organize their internal processes to convert scientific discoveries into viable technological solutions and market opportunities. In doing so, it emphasizes the strategic importance of aligning value-generating activities with the firm's innovation strategy and long-term competitive positioning.

MANAGEMENT OF VALUE-GENERATING ACTIVITIES

The management of value-generating activities within the biotech sector constitutes a complex process involving multiple players, resources, competencies, and development phases (Grant & Phene, 2022). The breadth and heterogeneity of biotechnological innovation, ranging from fundamental scientific discoveries to the market launch of products or services, require a sequence of interrelated activities, namely research, experimentation, development, production, IP protection, marketing, and distribution. In a highly competitive environment where development timelines can extend beyond a decade, and the risks associated with experimental failure or regulatory shifts are significant, biotech firms must exercise rigorous oversight over each activity of this process to maximize value creation and optimize resource allocation (Porter, 1985; Teece, 2018).

The primary analytical framework for examining value-creating activities within firms is the value chain, as introduced by Porter (1985). The value chain is a strategic construct that describes the full range of activities undertaken by a firm, which, when integrated effectively, contributes to the creation of value for the end customer. This analytical tool enables a detailed examination of a firm's internal operations and facilitates the identification of sources of sustainable competitive advantage. According to Porter, the value chain consists of two principal categories of activities (Fig. **16**), called primary activities and support activities.

Primary activities are directly involved in the creation, production, delivery, and distribution of the product or service. These include inbound logistics, production operations, outbound logistics, marketing and sales, and post-sale services. Support activities, on the other hand, include procurement management, technology development, human resource management, and corporate infrastructure. These activities provide essential support to the primary activities.

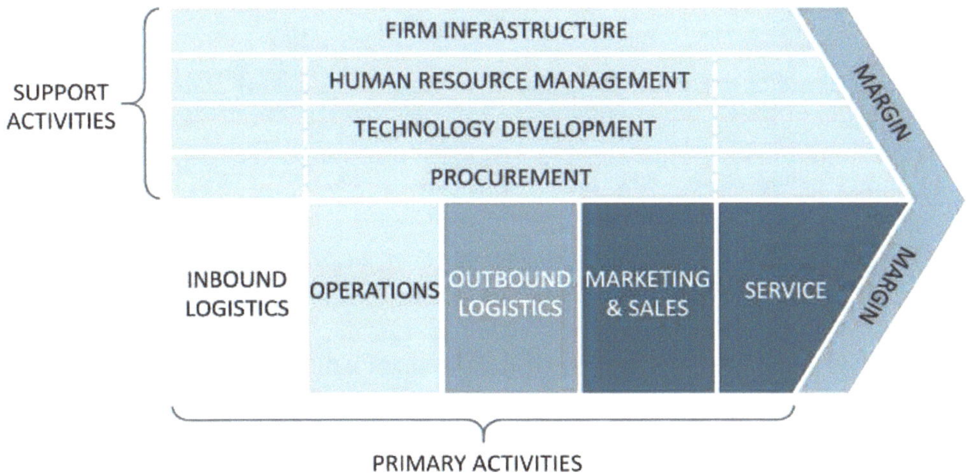

Fig. (16). Value chain tool (Porter, 1985).

In biotech firms, support activities play a decisive role in enabling primary activities to generate sustainable competitive advantage (Finegold & Frenkel, 2006). The academic literature on the value chain framework clearly indicates that excellence in primary activities depends heavily on the quality and efficiency of supporting managerial processes (Enginoğlu & Arikan, 2016; Porter, 1985).

Infrastructure Activities

Infrastructure activities primarily concern corporate governance, strategic and marketing planning, sustainability policies, management control systems, administration, financial management, institutional relations, and legal affairs. In biotech firms, corporate governance is often structured around integrating strategic and marketing planning processes with sustainability-related decisions and policies. This alignment is crucial to ensure that the research pipeline, which is typically capital-intensive, remains coherent with the firm's strategic objectives and with the ethical and environmental standards demanded by institutional stakeholders. At the same time, a formalized system of planning and management control, supported by administrative, financial, institutional, and legal functions, is essential to transform scientific achievements into credible assets for investors, industrial partners, and regulatory authorities. This process reduces operational risk while facilitating effective technology transfer (Cabaleiro-Cerviño & Mendi, 2024; Vurro *et al.*, 2024), as further highlighted in the following sections.

Human Resource Management

Human resource management consists of a set of sub-activities, commonly referred to as personnel policies. These include recruitment and selection, training, performance and potential evaluation, career development, compensation and incentive schemes, and industrial relations. In knowledge-based firms, attracting and retaining laboratory scientists, biostatisticians, regulatory affairs specialists, and business developers requires implementing incentive systems, creating interdisciplinary career paths, and promoting a corporate culture aligned with the firm's strategic orientation. According to the Resource-Based View (RBV) (Barney, 2001; Barney, Ketchen & Wright, 2021), rare and inimitable competencies can become a source of competitive advantage only if the firm can preserve them and facilitate cumulative learning. Consequently, continuous training programs, effective sharing of data and information within project teams, and internal mobility between scientific and managerial functions should be regarded as strategic investments to support the development and consolidation of organizational knowledge and capabilities.

Technology Development

Technology development refers to the generation of knowledge and the introduction of process and product innovations (Grant, 2002). Within a biotech firm, technology development extends well beyond laboratory research. For example, the adoption of omics platforms, the use of digital twins to simulate bioproduction processes, and the integration of AI algorithms into R&D workflows serve to optimize experimental cycles and create new opportunities for licensing. When supported by robust data governance frameworks, these digital infrastructures become reusable assets that can be applied across multiple projects. This not only reduces the costs of future experimentation but also enhances the firm's attractiveness to external partners seeking access to complementary technological platforms.

Procurement

Procurement involves the analysis and selection of suppliers, the management of supplier relationships, and the acquisition of goods and services required for production, service delivery, and other operational activities (Dullaeret *et al.*, 2025). For a firm that frequently outsources production to contract development and manufacturing organizations and clinical research to third-party firms, supplier selection encompasses not only raw materials (such as reagents) but also contractual clauses regarding data confidentiality, IP sharing, and compliance with governance, social, and environmental criteria. European policies on sustainability and the broader framework promoting zero-impact industry increasingly encourage firms to select partners capable of ensuring traceability of raw materials, reducing emissions, and promoting fair labor practices. Attention to these factors, in turn, facilitates access to public funding opportunities and to investment capital oriented towards sustainability goals.

Inbound Logistics

Inbound logistics includes planning and coordinating supplier deliveries, managing carriers for inbound shipments, physically receiving materials, conducting compliance checks, allocating received items to designated storage areas, and administering raw material and semi-finished goods inventories. In biotech firms, inbound logistics also involves the acquisition and management of all research-related inputs: biological samples, high-purity reagents, molecular data from genomic repositories, and, not infrequently, licensed rights to patented sequences. The quality of these materials, the ethical traceability of their origins, and the timeliness of their delivery to laboratory facilities directly affect the reliability of experimental results and compliance with good research and production practices (González-Sánchez, Alonso-Munoz & Kocollari, 2025; Júnior, Frederico & Costa, 2019).

Operations (Production and Core Activities)

Operations include all activities related to preparing facilities, organizing the production or service delivery cycle, and transforming inputs into outputs. These are complemented by equipment validation, quality control procedures, and the transfer of outputs to outbound storage. Operations represent the strategic core of the entire process, extending from the identification of therapeutic targets to the production of batches for clinical trials and, subsequently, to commercial-scale production in environments compliant with Good Manufacturing Practices. Within this operational perimeter are also included analytical characterization, stability testing, preparation of regulatory dossiers, and interactions with health authorities. Every product- or process-related decision, from the choice of cell line to the purification methodology, has significant implications for both cost and time, ultimately influencing the speed at which a molecule advances through the various development stages (McGlinchey *et al.*, 2025).

Outbound Logistics

This activity involves the management of finished goods warehouses, the planning and coordination of deliveries to distributors, the handling of outbound products, and the fulfillment of customer orders. In biotech firms, outbound logistics takes on two distinct forms. During clinical trials, it entails the secure and traceable distribution of investigational drugs to the research centers involved, requiring, for example, strict adherence to cold chain logistics and documentation that complies with Good Clinical Practice standards. Once marketing authorization has been obtained, for firms engaged in production, this function shifts to coordinating distribution flows to wholesalers, hospital pharmacies, and, in some cases, national distributors, ensuring continuity and reliability in the supply chain (Peng & Liao, 2025).

Marketing and Sales

Marketing and sales refer to the four fundamental levers through which a firm manages its market offering: product or service, pricing, distribution channels, and communication strategies. In biotech firms, this activity goes far beyond mere product or service promotion. It includes negotiating pricing and reimbursement terms with payor agencies, disseminating clinical evidence to prescribing physicians, and implementing medical affairs initiatives that support therapy adoption through real-world data. Since the profile of the customer changes over the course of the product life cycle, from venture capital investors to regulatory authorities, and ultimately to national healthcare providers, the firm's value narrative must continuously adapt. This requires a delicate balance between promises of efficacy, economic and environmental sustainability, and social responsibility.

Services

The service activity refers specifically to post-sale actions. These include post-sale support, customer satisfaction monitoring, management of customer relationships, and the provision of supplementary services intended to increase the perceived value of the product or service (such as warranty coverage). In the context of biotech firms, post-sale service activities include pharmacovigilance, scientific support for clinicians and end users, phase IV clinical studies, and logistical support for advanced therapies that require personalized administration. This same activity also involves collecting real-world outcome data, which feeds into a virtuous cycle of learning. Such a cycle may lead to expanded therapeutic indications or to process improvements (Enginoğlu & Arikan, 2016; Prahalad & Hamel, 1999).

Interdependence of Primary and Supporting Activities

Taken as a whole, primary activities should not be understood as routine operational mechanisms. Rather, they determine a biotech firm's capacity to transform laboratory discoveries into tangible therapeutic benefits, while meeting timelines, cost objectives, and regulatory requirements. It is the quality of execution in these activities that ultimately crystallizes sustainable competitive advantage, in accordance with the logic underlying the value chain framework. Moreover, the interdependence both among support activities and between support and primary activities constitutes a fundamental multiplier of value. For example, governance models that reward transparency in clinical data foster an internal culture of information sharing, which in turn accelerates learning time among research teams. The development of digital platforms enhances visibility across critical suppliers and reduces the risk of supply chain disruptions. Contractual frameworks that integrate patent protection with environmental requirements reinforce both the firm's reputation and its access to sustainability-linked financing instruments.

A board of directors capable of integrating strategic planning, regulatory risk management, and financial oversight, and oriented toward a variety of exit strategies, enables more effective capital allocation to the most promising research projects. Likewise, the proactive management of IP, including competitor patent surveillance and the negotiation of inbound and outbound licensing agreements, transforms tacit laboratory knowledge into a negotiable asset that can generate early cash flows and attract strategic partners.

What emerges from this analysis is that support activities act as strategic levers that enable the conversion of rapid scientific innovation into economic, social, and ethical value, thereby strengthening the firm's long-term competitive position.

RESOURCES AND COMPETENCIES

The relationship between the value chain and competitive advantage is closely tied to the firm's ability to perform certain activities more effectively than its competitors or at a lower cost. Competitive advantage can take two principal forms: cost advantage, when the firm performs similar activities at a lower cost than its competitors; and differentiation advantage, when the firm offers greater value to customers through unique features of its product or service.

From this perspective, internal resources and competencies play a decisive role in acquiring and sustaining competitive advantage (Grant, 2020). Resources can be classified as tangible (*e.g.*, physical infrastructure, financial capital, and technological assets) and intangible (*e.g.*, human resources, brand equity, patents, and corporate reputation). These resources constitute the material and immaterial foundation upon which the firm can structure and execute its value-creating activities. Table 7 presents a detailed analysis of the key resources in a biotech firm.

Competencies represent the organizational capabilities through which resources are effectively integrated to generate value. In fact, for the attainment of competitive advantage, organizational capabilities of integration and coordination are essential to the development of the corporate system (Fontana & Caroli, 2013). Through the coordination and integration of internal resources, whether tangible, intangible, human, or financial, as well as external resources, the firm gives rise to a set of competencies that, in turn, can generate new resources. This dynamic illustrates one manifestation of a firm's autopoietic capacity. Autopoiesis refers to a firm's ability to continuously redefine itself, sustaining and reproducing its structure through its own resources and competencies (Prahalad & Hamel, 1999).

Table 7. Articulation of key resources in a biotech firm (own elaboration).

Type of Resource	Corresponding Elements in Biotech Companies
Tangible	Certified laboratories; biosafety infrastructures; facilities (*e.g.*, pilot bioproduction lines with single-use bioreactors and purification systems); high-precision analytical instruments and technologies (*e.g.*, mass spectrometers and next-generation sequencers).
Intangible	*Knowledge*: know-how; tacit and explicit knowledge. *Technologies*: patent portfolios; AI platforms; proprietary algorithms; omics databases; biobanks of biological samples. *Reputational*: brand equity; credibility with scientific and academic communities, public and private investors, regulatory authorities; track record of completed clinical studies and research projects *Relational*: Established collaborations with universities, healthcare providers, hospitals, research centers, pharmaceutical and biotech companies; participation in regional clusters and scientific research networks at local, national, and international levels.
Financial	Liquidity from venture capital, dedicated public funds, tax credits, and non-repayable research grants; funding from National, European, and international programs.
Human Resources	*Specialist resources*: researchers experienced in the specific sector/sub-sector of reference. ***Cross-functional resources:*** Personnel experienced in regulatory affairs; Personnel experienced in project management; Personnel experienced in digital technologies.

Competencies may vary in nature, ranging from technological and productive to commercial or managerial, and not all hold the same degree of importance in the context of business management. Competencies are defined as distinctive when they serve as the foundation of a firm's competitive advantage, as they are difficult to acquire and replicate. These competencies have also been identified by Prahalad & Hamel (1999) as core competencies and as the fundamental competencies for building a firm's competitive positioning.

Core competencies are characterized by three essential attributes: i) they contribute to the value created by the firm and to the efficiency in the delivery of the product or service; ii) they represent the key competitive factor within a specific business domain; iii) they are difficult for competitors to imitate.

In biotech firms, three core domains of competency can be identified: primary R&D activities (specialized competencies), human resource management, and technology development. Given the characteristics of the macro-environment and the competitive context (see Chapter 1), it is also possible to identify three additional areas of competency that contribute to the establishment of a sustainable competitive position, which are the management of IORs (relational competencies), stakeholder management, and the sustainable strategic management (sustainability-related competencies) (Kim, 2019).

Through a rigorous analysis of the value chain, a firm can identify which internal activities may be improved or further enhanced, thereby defining strategies to maximize the potential of its resources and core competencies in alignment with the opportunities and threats in both the macro-environment and the specific sector. This process fosters a virtuous learning cycle that supports effective strategic management and the achievement of a sustainable competitive position over time.

CONCLUDING REMARKS

The examination of value-generating activities in biotech firms highlights the central role of effective coordination across the various stages of the value chain. From the acquisition of research inputs and the organization of laboratory activities to production, distribution, and post-sale support, each phase contributes to transforming scientific knowledge into tangible economic and social value.

In this context, the value chain framework offers an effective analytical tool for understanding how competitive advantage emerges from the integration of primary and support activities. Primary activities -such as operations, logistics, marketing interfaces, and service provision- are strongly dependent on the quality and efficiency of supporting functions, including corporate governance, human resource management, technological development, and procurement strategies.

The analysis also highlights the importance of internal resources and organizational capabilities in sustaining long-term competitive advantage.

Tangible assets, such as laboratories and technological infrastructures, interact with intangible resources, including intellectual capital, scientific reputation, relational networks, and proprietary technologies. By integrating these elements, biotech firms develop distinctive competencies that are difficult for competitors to replicate.

In highly knowledge-intensive environments, the capacity to coordinate resources and competencies becomes a critical determinant of strategic success. Firms that effectively align their value-generating activities with their scientific capabilities and strategic objectives are better positioned to manage complex innovation processes, control regulatory costs, and sustain long development cycles. Consequently, competitive advantage in biotechnology does not depend solely on scientific breakthroughs but also on the organizational capability to orchestrate the resources and activities required to transform research outcomes into reliable products, services, and technological platforms.

CHAPTER 5

Strategic Marketing, Intellectual Property, and Sustainable Value Creation

Abstract: This chapter explores how biotechnology firms translate scientific innovation into sustainable economic and societal value through strategic marketing and effective intellectual property management. In knowledge-intensive sectors, marketing serves as a governance function, supporting technology transfer, stakeholder communication, and the positioning of innovation within complex scientific and industrial ecosystems. The chapter examines how intellectual property portfolios strengthen firms' competitive advantage by protecting technological discoveries while enabling licensing agreements, collaborative development projects, and strategic alliances. It also highlights the growing importance of stakeholder engagement and transparent communication with investors, regulatory authorities, research institutions, and healthcare organizations. Finally, the chapter analyzes the contribution of biotechnology firms to sustainable development, emphasizing their role in addressing global challenges related to health, environmental protection, agriculture, and industrial transformation. By integrating innovation management, marketing strategies, and sustainability-oriented governance, biotech firms demonstrate how economic performance and societal value creation can reinforce each other in the knowledge economy.

Keywords: Intellectual property, Strategic marketing, Stakeholder engagement, Sustainable innovation, SDGs, Technology transfer.

INTRODUCTION

Building upon the analysis of innovation processes and value-generating activities presented in the previous chapters, this chapter explores how biotech firms translate scientific and technological capabilities into sustainable market value. In knowledge-intensive industries, the commercialization of innovation requires not only strong research capabilities and efficient organizational processes but also effective strategies for intellectual property management, stakeholder engagement, and market positioning.

In the biotech sector, marketing assumes a distinctive strategic role. Rather than being limited to promotional activities, it operates as a governance function that

Paola Olimpia Achard

supports the communication of scientific value, facilitates technology transfer processes, and strengthens relationships with a wide range of stakeholders, including investors, research institutions, healthcare organizations, regulatory authorities, and industrial partners.

Within this perspective, intellectual property represents one of the most critical strategic assets for biotech firms. Patents, proprietary technologies, and specialized know-how not only protect innovation outcomes but also create opportunities for licensing agreements, collaborative development projects, and strategic alliances. The management and valorization of intellectual property, therefore, become central elements in the broader process of innovation commercialization.

Finally, the chapter examines the growing relevance of sustainability and social responsibility within the strategic orientation of biotech firms. By developing solutions to global challenges in healthcare, agriculture, environmental protection, and industrial processes, the biotech sector directly contributes to several Sustainable Development Goals (SDGs). In this context, integrating innovation management, marketing strategies, and sustainability-oriented governance enables biotech firms to generate economic value while simultaneously fostering broader societal and environmental benefits.

STRATEGIC MARKETING FOR INNOVATION: CREATION, MANAGEMENT, AND VALORIZATION OF INTELLECTUAL PROPERTY

Today, marketing represents a core business function that plays a pivotal role in establishing and sustaining competitive advantage across many sectors. For a biotech firm, irrespective of the specific subsector, recognizing R&D as the fundamental business activity requires framing marketing as a governance function, including knowledge management, corporate reputation, and technology transfer processes, rather than limiting it to a set of promotional and distribution tactics.

Within marketing activities, a clear distinction exists between strategic dimensions, such as market segmentation, brand positioning, and brand management, and operational dimensions, which include pricing, product and service management, as well as communication and distribution channel decisions. In the context of biotech firms, strategic marketing and the management and valorization of IP should not be treated as separate disciplines, but rather as interconnected components of a value creation strategy. A well-developed IP portfolio enhances the firm's competitive positioning and bargaining power. Concurrently, effective communication about the firm's innovative potential, supported by scientific publications and strategic partnerships, increases the appeal of the IP portfolio to key stakeholders, including investors and licensees. Consequently, developing a product and service pipeline requires a dual assessment of profitability and patent defensibility, carefully balancing research projects by their degree of innovation. Every decision, ranging from project selection and licensing of ancillary technologies to the establishment of spin-offs or joint ventures with partners, has direct implications for the firm's financial health and the value proposition presented to stakeholders (Fahy & Smithee, 1999; Varadarajan, 2010). Technology transfer is therefore a critical activity that mitigates financial risk while simultaneously fostering trust among investors, regulatory authorities, healthcare organizations, and potential licensees. Rather than awaiting the commercial phase, the firm progressively builds external validation that enhances its credibility (Grupp & Gaines-Ross, 2002; Hunt & Hansen, 2010).

Applying foundational marketing principles requires the continuous adjustment of the value proposition. This may involve promoting exit strategies to forward-thinking financiers, disseminating robust clinical evidence to industrial partners, and presenting data on therapeutic efficacy and economic, social, and ethical sustainability to reimbursement bodies (Palmatier & Crecelius, 2019). Additionally, the dynamics of the biotech macro-environment (political, institutional, technological, and legal factors outlined in Chapter 1) alongside an emphasis on collaboration, smart specialization, and the integration of environmental and social criteria in innovation projects, require that corporate reputation be strategically managed to facilitate access to public funding and establish long-term partnerships (Sheth & Parvatiyar, 2021). At the same time, strategic marketing aims to systematically convert research outcomes into viable market opportunities, building credibility through transparent, consistent communication grounded in accessible, verifiable data. For biotech firms, this often entails not merely promoting an existing product or service but highlighting the potential therapeutic, environmental, social, and ethical benefits that innovations under development promise to deliver to healthcare systems, the biotech and pharmaceutical sectors, and society. Communication strategies must be tailored to specific stakeholders. For example, the scientific community requires detailed research methodologies and protocols, investors need clear visibility on project phases and associated capital deployment, while healthcare providers seek compelling evidence of efficacy and safety.

Fig. (**17**) depicts marketing of biotech firms as an ecosystem orchestration process. The biotech firm is positioned at the center and interacts with key stakeholders, *i.e.*, research institutions, hospitals, regulators, agencies, investors, patients, advocacy groups, and industry partners, through various activities including technology scouting, evidence generation, market access, stakeholder engagement, and alliance management.

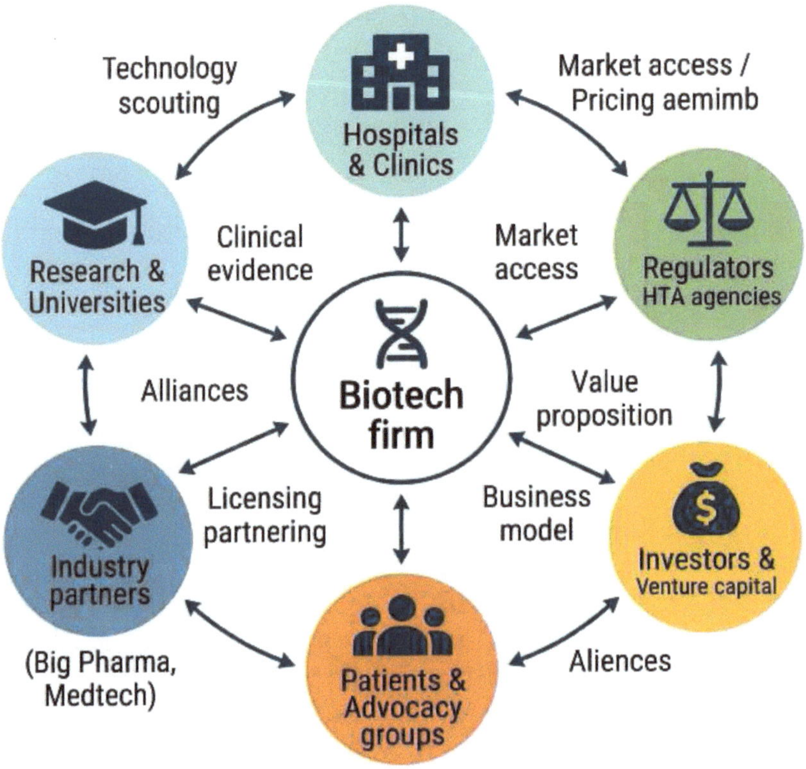

Fig. (17). Marketing as ecosystem orchestration in a biotech firm (own elaboration).

Within this framework, technology licensing and co-development agreements structured with defined milestones and options to continue upon successful achievement become essential marketing tools. These arrangements facilitate cost and risk sharing and multiply opportunities for external validation. Simultaneously, protecting IP through targeted patent filings and proactive legal strategies supports the firm's competitive positioning. Participation in conferences, seminars, and scientific forums, along with professional collaborations, fosters a reputation that links scientific rigor with ethical integrity.

The integrated management of technology portfolios, scientific communication, stakeholder engagement, and IP valorization and protection enables biotech firms to translate innovation into sustainable long-term value creation, balancing economic, environmental, ethical, and social impact.

THE CONTRIBUTION OF BIOTECH FIRMS TO SUSTAINABLE DEVELOPMENT

Biotech firms integrate strategic responses to scientific challenges and social needs, thanks to their distinctive anatomy: knowledge intensity, intra- and intersectoral networks, and strong solution scalability. These features position them among the key players in pursuing the SDGs (Bade *et al.*, 2024; Cabaleiro-Cerviño & Mendi, 2024; United Nations, 2015). Biotech firms have a systemic impact, particularly on SDG #3 (Health) and SDG #9 (Innovation). However, their positive effects extend to nearly all 17 SDGs in the 2030 Agenda. This is evidenced by the mapping developed by the International Council of Biotechnology Associations (Table **8**), which highlights contributions ranging from combating hunger to climate action, as well as water conservation and clean energy (Biocat, 2023; Etit *et al.*, 2024).

Table 8. Biotech firms' contribution to SDGs (own elaboration based on International Council of Biotechnology Association, 2023).

SDG *vs* biotechnology contribution	
SDG#1 - Biotechnology helps farmers increase income and reduce their vulnerability to climate change.	SDG#9 - Biotechnology R&D is empowering scientists to develop solutions to the most pressing global challenges.
SDG#2 - Agricultural biotechnology is critical in helping to feed a growing world population.	SDG#12 - Industrial Biotechnology applies tools to traditional processes to produce more sustainable products and materials.
SDG#3 - Biotechnology plays a critical role in saving lives and improving the quality of life for all.	SDG#13 - Biotechnology's agricultural and industrial applications are critical in combating the effects of climate change.
SDG#6 - Biotechnology helps ensure the availability and sustainable management of water and sanitation.	SDG#14 - Biotechnology can contribute to efforts to conserve and sustainably use ocean resources.
SDG#7 - Biofuels derived from a range of renewable sources reduce CO_2 in transportation fuels.	SDG#15 - Agricultural Biotechnology innovation contributes to the protection of terrestrial ecosystems and biodiversity.
SDG#8 - Biotechnology innovations present opportunities for economic growth.	SDG#17 – Biotech firms, NGOs, research, and multilateral institutions and governments are creating global partnerships.

The value generated by biotech firms is not solely in the molecules, biofertilizers, or biopolymers they bring to market. Rather, it lies primarily in how they coordinate knowledge, stakeholders, and governance. Managing innovation through the lens of Corporate Social Responsibility involves combining competitiveness with social and environmental impact, reengineering value chain activities using circular economy principles, and integrating SDGs metrics into planning, control, and incentive systems. This approach activates virtuous cycles of shared value creation that reinforce competitive advantage while generating broad benefits for the community and the environment (Cabaleiro-Cerviño & Mendi, 2024; Dullaert *et al.*, 2025).

Evidence from leading global players shows a clear evolution toward this model. AbbVie (USA), for example, has doubled its workforce to over 50,000 employees across seventy countries, with 52% of managerial roles held by women and roughly one-fifth of employees directly engaged in R&D. Cultural and gender diversity is treated as a key enabler of innovation, while more than 250 partnerships with competitors, universities, and NGOs support the dissemination of expertise and scalability of solutions. Novo Nordisk (Denmark) links the performance of over 2,300 employees to combined financial, social, and environmental goals, regularly involving around 500 key stakeholders in assessment phases. This approach merges financial performance with impact measurement, ensuring transparency in aligning corporate purpose with the SDG taxonomy (Bruneo *et al.*, 2024; Gucciardi, 2024; Vurro *et al.*, 2024). A similar commitment to shared value creation characterizes CSL (Australia). The firm has established an Executive Committee for Sustainability reporting directly to the CEO and segments its stakeholders into key categories: internal, external, primary, and institutional. This segmentation helps calibrate engagement on material issues. Patients, the most relevant primary stakeholder group, participate in research pathways and co-design the modalities to access the therapy. Plasma donors and scientific partners engage in safety, quality, and collaboration strategies, including open innovation.

Beyond the social and relational dimensions, biotech firms have evolved more strategically to apply stringent ethical criteria across their supply chains. For instance, Amgen (USA) requires each supplier to provide substantial, not merely formal, evidence of adherence to its Supplier Code of Conduct, which covers human rights, safety, environment, and transparency. Responsibility thus extends upstream and downstream in the value chain, transforming the entire supply chain into a vehicle for positive impact and risk reduction. Regeneron reinforces this vision with a Code of Conduct focused on clinical data sharing, animal welfare, and quality traceability. Ethics is therefore a cornerstone of its R&D processes (Lowe *et al.*, 2016).

The environmental dimension shows how sustainability can serve as an operational driver of excellence. Vertex (USA) has established cross-functional committees overseeing emission reduction, water conservation, waste minimization, and the adoption of green chemistry practices. This demonstrates that climate action and industrial productivity can reinforce each other. Bristol Myers Squibb (USA) pushes this paradigm further by applying sustainability criteria to strategic partner selection, packaging, and logistics choices. The aim is to reduce the dispersion of active pharmaceutical ingredients into the environment and to decarbonize critical stages of the drug life cycle (Dullaert *et al.*, 2025; Etit *et al.*, 2024).

In governance, Roche (Switzerland) serves as a benchmark for multi-level sustainability integration. A complex system of committees, from the Board to the Corporate Sustainability Steering Committee and the Global Network of Subsidiaries, ensures strategic direction, operational implementation, and reporting mutually reinforce each other, covering economic, social, environmental, and ethical dimensions simultaneously. Within this structure, sustainability is not an accessory function, but a management orientation embedded across every business area and organizational unit (Bade *et al.*, 2024; Vurro *et al.*, 2024).

Ultimately, the emerging trajectory is of a sector capable of transforming sustainability from a constraint into a strategic driver. By integrating the SDGs into corporate purpose, redesigning innovation processes, and structuring governance to enable measurable shared value creation, biotech firms demonstrate that economic development and socio-environmental progress are synergistic outcomes. The convergence of frontier science, widespread responsibility, and global-local partnerships fuels an inclusive innovation cycle that reduces environmental footprint, expands healthcare access, enhances human resource value, and strengthens territorial resilience.

CONCLUDING REMARKS

The analysis presented in this chapter highlights the essential role of strategic marketing and effective intellectual property management in translating scientific innovation into sustainable value creation. In highly knowledge-intensive sectors, marketing cannot be limited to traditional promotional activities; rather, it serves as a governance mechanism that coordinates technology transfer processes, stakeholder communication, and the firm's strategic positioning within complex innovation ecosystems.

A well-structured intellectual property portfolio strengthens the firm’s competitive position by protecting technological discoveries and enabling the development of licensing agreements, strategic alliances, and co-development partnerships. At the same time, transparent communication with investors, regulatory authorities, scientific communities, and healthcare institutions helps build credibility and facilitate access to financial resources and collaborative opportunities.

Beyond economic performance, the role of biotech firms increasingly extends to generating broader social and environmental value. By developing innovative solutions across healthcare, agriculture, environmental protection, and industrial biotechnology, the sector directly contributes to several SDGs. In this perspective, sustainability becomes not only an ethical commitment but also a strategic driver that guides corporate decision-making and reinforces long-term competitiveness.

The integration of innovation management, stakeholder engagement, and sustainability-oriented governance, therefore, outlines a model of strategic value creation in which scientific progress, economic development, and social responsibility converge. In this evolving landscape, biotech firms demonstrate that effective alignment of knowledge, governance, and collaborative networks can foster virtuous cycles of innovation that generate lasting benefits for the economy and society.

GENERAL CONCLUSION

The analyses developed throughout this volume have highlighted how the strategic management of biotechnology firms must be understood within the broader transformation of contemporary knowledge-based economies. Biotechnology represents one of the most paradigmatic sectors in which scientific discovery, technological development, and market creation are deeply interconnected. In such contexts, competitive advantage does not emerge solely from technological breakthroughs but from the firm's ability to strategically organize knowledge, resources, and collaborative networks to transform scientific potential into sustainable economic and societal value.

The first part of the book has shown how the external environment plays a decisive role in shaping the strategic trajectories of biotech firms. Political orientations, regulatory frameworks, technological infrastructures, and financial ecosystems jointly define the opportunity space within which firms operate. In knowledge-intensive sectors characterized by high uncertainty and long development cycles, firms must continuously align their strategic choices with institutional dynamics, innovation policies, and evolving technological paradigms. As a result, competitiveness increasingly depends on the capacity to navigate complex regulatory environments and to position the firm within dynamic innovation ecosystems.

The second dimension explored in this volume concerns the strategic role of interorganizational collaborations. Biotechnology firms rarely innovate in isolation. Instead, they operate within dense networks that connect universities, research centers, pharmaceutical companies, venture capital investors, and public institutions. Strategic alliances, research partnerships, and innovation networks, therefore, become essential mechanisms for accessing complementary knowledge, sharing risks, and accelerating technological development. These collaborative arrangements also represent a crucial pathway for emerging firms to scale their innovation trajectories and integrate into global value chains. Building upon this external and relational perspective, the analysis has then focused on the internal strategic architecture of biotech firms. Business models constitute a central mechanism through which firms organize innovation processes and structure the transformation of scientific discoveries into technological platforms, therapeutic applications, or industrial solutions. The diversity of business model configurations -from dedicated research-oriented firms to more integrated structures- reflects different strategic responses to the challenges of uncertainty, financing constraints, and regulatory complexity. In all cases, however, the effective alignment between scientific capabilities, organizational structures, and collaborative ecosystems emerges as a key determinant of long-term competitiveness. The examination of value-generating activities has further emphasized that the strategic performance of biotech firms depends on the effective integration of the entire value chain. From research inputs and experimental development to production, regulatory validation, and market access, each phase requires the coordination of specialized resources and organizational competencies. Tangible assets, such as laboratories and technological infrastructure, interact with intangible resources, including intellectual capital, scientific reputation, relational networks, and proprietary technologies. By integrating these elements, firms develop distinctive competencies that enable them to manage complex innovation processes and sustain competitive advantage over time.

Paola Olimpia Achard

Finally, the analysis has highlighted that the commercialization of biotechnology innovation increasingly requires integrating strategic marketing, intellectual property management, and stakeholder engagement. In knowledge-intensive industries, marketing functions extend far beyond traditional product promotion. Instead, they operate as governance mechanisms that support technology transfer, facilitate communication with investors and regulators, and position innovation within broader scientific and industrial ecosystems. Intellectual property portfolios represent a strategic asset that allows firms to protect discoveries while simultaneously enabling licensing strategies, collaborative agreements, and new forms of technological diffusion.

Taken together, the different dimensions analyzed in this book suggest that biotechnology firms operate at the intersection of science, strategy, and societal transformation. The capacity to integrate research excellence, organizational capabilities, and collaborative governance determines not only the success of individual firms but also the broader evolution of innovation ecosystems in which they are embedded.

From a managerial perspective, the findings underline the importance of adopting integrated strategic approaches that combine innovation management, resource orchestration, and collaborative governance. Managers operating in biotechnology firms must develop capabilities not only in scientific and technological domains but also in alliance management, regulatory navigation, and strategic communication with diverse stakeholder groups. In such environments, competitive advantage increasingly depends on the ability to coordinate interdisciplinary knowledge and to structure innovation processes capable of sustaining long-term development trajectories.

The different dimensions examined throughout this volume also highlight the increasingly central role played by biotechnology innovation ecosystems. Biotech firms rarely operate as isolated entities; rather, they are embedded in complex, evolving systems of relationships that connect universities, research centers, pharmaceutical and technology companies, venture capital investors, healthcare institutions, and public authorities. Within these ecosystems, knowledge circulates across organizational and disciplinary boundaries, enabling the recombination of scientific discoveries, technological capabilities, and entrepreneurial initiatives. Strategic positioning within such ecosystems, therefore, becomes a critical determinant of long-term competitiveness. Firms that can orchestrate collaborative networks, access distributed knowledge sources, and actively participate in innovation clusters are better positioned to accelerate discovery and translate research outcomes into scalable technological solutions.

Looking ahead, the future trajectory of biotechnology is likely to be shaped by several transformative dynamics. First, the rapid integration of AI and advanced data analytics into research processes is redefining the discovery and development paradigms of the life sciences. Data-driven experimentation, machine learning models applied to genomic and clinical datasets, and digital platforms that integrate biological and computational knowledge are progressively transforming how innovation is generated and managed. Second, the increasing availability of large-scale biological data -from genomics and proteomics to real-world clinical evidence- is reinforcing the strategic importance of data governance and interdisciplinary competencies combining biology, informatics, and engineering. At the same time, biotechnology is expected to play an increasingly strategic role in addressing some of the most pressing global challenges. Advances in biomedical research, sustainable agriculture, bio-based industrial processes, and environmental biotechnology offer significant opportunities to improve global health, mitigate climate change, and support the transition to more sustainable production systems. In this context, the alignment between scientific innovation, sustainability objectives, and responsible governance is likely to become a defining feature of the sector's future evolution.

For both managers and policy makers, these transformations imply the need to rethink traditional approaches to innovation and industrial strategy. Strengthening research infrastructures, facilitating interdisciplinary collaboration, supporting technology transfer mechanisms, and fostering international partnerships will be essential to fully exploit the potential of biotechnology innovation. Ultimately, the future of the sector will depend on the capacity of firms, institutions, and societies to collectively govern the complex interactions between science, technology, markets, and public interests, ensuring that the extraordinary potential of biotechnology contributes not only to economic competitiveness but also to broader societal well-being.

REFERENCES

Abell, D.F. (1980). *Defining the business: The starting point of strategic planning.* Prentice-Hall.

Achard, P.O., Bellini, C. (2023). Value creation processes in the European biotech industry: The role of collaboration strategies. *Proceedings of the ERAZ Conference: Knowledge-Based Sustainable Development,* 91-108.
[http://dx.doi.org/10.31410/ERAZ.S.P.2023.63]

Achard, P.O., Bellini, C., Ioannucci, L. (2025). Case of innovative governance of IRCCS. *Proceedings of the 45th Eurasia Business and Economics Society Conference,* 91-102.
[http://dx.doi.org/10.1007/978-3-031-80256-0_6]

Addy, N., Dubé, L. (2018). Addressing complex societal problems: Enabling multiple dimensions of proximity to sustain partnerships for collective impact in Quebec. *Sustainability (Basel), 10*(4), 980.
[http://dx.doi.org/10.3390/su10040980]

Ahn, M.J., Meeks, M. (2008). Building a conducive environment for life science-based entrepreneurship and industry clusters. *J. Commer. Biotechnol, 14*(1), 20-30.
[http://dx.doi.org/10.1057/palgrave.jcb.3050076]

Arden, N.S., Fisher, A.C., Tyner, K., Yu, L.X., Lee, S.L., Kopcha, M. (2021). Industry 4.0 for pharmaceutical manufacturing: Preparing for the smart factories of the future. *Int. J. Pharm, 602*, 120554.
[http://dx.doi.org/10.1016/j.ijpharm.2021.120554] [PMID: 33794326]

Arora, A., Fosfuri, A., Gambardella, A. (2001). Specialized technology suppliers, international spillovers and investment: evidence from the chemical industry. *J. Dev. Econ, 65*(1), 31-54.
[http://dx.doi.org/10.1016/S0304-3878(01)00126-2]

Arsawan, I.W.E., Koval, V., Rajiani, I., Rustiarini, N.W., Supartha, W.G., Suryantini, N.P.S. (2022). Leveraging knowledge sharing and innovation culture into SMEs sustainable competitive advantage. *Int. J. Prod. Perform. Manag, 71*(2), 405-428.
[http://dx.doi.org/10.1108/IJPPM-04-2020-0192]

AseBio. (2024). Informe AseBio 2024: Hacia una Europa más competitiva *Asociación Española de Bioempresas.* Available from: https://www.asebio.com/informe-asebio-2024

Ashley, E.A. (2016). Towards precision medicine. *Nat. Rev. Genet, 17*(9), 507-522.
[http://dx.doi.org/10.1038/nrg.2016.86] [PMID: 27528417]

Assobiotec–Federchimica. (2023). *BioInItaly report 2023: The Italian biotech industry – Economic update 2023.* Available from: https://assobiotec.federchimica.it/docs/default-source/default-document-library/bioinitaly-report-2023.pdf [accessed 31 March 2026].

Aulkemeier, F., Iacob, M.E., van Hillegersberg, J. (2019). Platform-based collaboration in digital ecosystems. *Electron. Mark, 29*(4), 597-608.
[http://dx.doi.org/10.1007/s12525-019-00341-2]

Bade, C., Olsacher, A., Boehme, P., Truebel, H., Bürger, L., Fehring, L. (2024). Sustainability in the pharmaceutical industry—An assessment of SUSTAINABILITY maturity and effects of SUSTAINABILITY measure implementation on supply chain security. *Corp. Soc. Resp. Environ. Manag, 31*(1), 224-242.

[http://dx.doi.org/10.1002/csr.2564]

Bailón, L., Llano, A., Cedeño, S., Escribà, T., Rosás-Umbert, M., Parera, M., Casadellà, M., Lopez, M., Pérez, F., Oriol-Tordera, B., Ruiz-Riol, M., Coll, J., Perez, F., Rivero, À., Leselbaum, A.R., McGowan, I., Sengupta, D., Wee, E.G., Hanke, T., Paredes, R., Alarcón-Soto, Y., Clotet, B., Noguera-Julian, M., Brander, C., Molto, J., Mothe, B., Barriocanal, A.M., Benet, S., Cobarsi, P., Geleziunas, R., Leselbaum, A.R., Loste, C., Meulbroek, M., Miranda, C., Muñoz, J., Naval, J., Nieto, A., Pujol, F., Puig, J. (2022). Safety, immunogenicity and effect on viral rebound of HTI vaccines in early treated HIV-1 infection: a randomized, placebo-controlled phase 1 trial. *Nat. Med, 28*(12), 2611-2621.
[http://dx.doi.org/10.1038/s41591-022-02060-2] [PMID: 36302893]

Baldwin, C. Y., Clark, K. B. (2000). *Design rules: Volume 1, The power of modularity.* MIT Press.
[http://dx.doi.org/10.7551/mitpress/2366.001.0001]

Barney, J.B. (2001). Resource-based theories of competitive advantage: A ten-year retrospective on the resource-based view. *J. Manage, 27*(6), 643-650.
[http://dx.doi.org/10.1177/014920630102700602]

Barney, J.B., Ketchen, D.J., Jr, Wright, M. (2021). Resource-based theory and the value creation framework. *J. Manage, 47*(7), 1936-1955.
[http://dx.doi.org/10.1177/01492063211021655]

Bianchi, M., Cavaliere, A., Chiaroni, D., Frattini, F., Chiesa, V. (2011). Organisational modes for Open Innovation in the bio-pharmaceutical industry: An exploratory analysis. *Technovation, 31*(1), 22-33.
[http://dx.doi.org/10.1016/j.technovation.2010.03.002]

Bigliardi, B., Nosella, A., Verbano, C. (2005). Business models in Italian biotechnology industry: a quantitative analysis. *Technovation, 25*(11), 1299-1306.
[http://dx.doi.org/10.1016/j.technovation.2004.10.013]

Biocat. (2023). *BioRegion of Catalonia report 2023: Life sciences and healthcare sector in Catalonia.* Available from: https://report.biocat.cat/docs/2023_Catalonia_BioRegion_Report.pdf?v=20240221_001 [accessed 31 March 2026].

BioIndustry Association. (2018). *A vision for the UK life sciences sector in 2025 (Reprint of 2015 report).* Available from: https://www.bioindustry.org/static/uploaded/61dae119-1172-45e3-b9b030fc6e6a9579.pdf [accessed 31 March 2026].

Biobased Industries Consortium. (2025) Annual report. Available from: https://biconsortium.eu/sites/biconsortium.eu/files/publications/BIC-2025-Annual-Report-interactive.pdf [accessed 31 March 2026].

Biotechnology Innovation Consortium. (2025). *Biotechnology Innovation Consortium.* Available from: https://biconsortium.eu [accessed 31 March 2026].

Bloem, V., Salimi, N. (2023). Role of knowledge management processes within different stages of technological innovation: evidence from biotechnology SMEs. *Knowl. Manag. Res. Pract, 21*(4), 822-836.
[http://dx.doi.org/10.1080/14778238.2022.2064352]

Borge, L., Bröring, S. (2020). What affects technology transfer in emerging knowledge areas? A multi-stakeholder concept mapping study in the bioeconomy. *J. Technol. Transf, 45*(2), 430-460.
[http://dx.doi.org/10.1007/s10961-018-9702-4]

Bourgeois, L.J. (1980). Strategy and environment: A conceptual integration. *Acad. Manage. Rev, 5*(1), 25-39.

[http://dx.doi.org/10.2307/257802]

Brandenburger, A.M., Nalebuff, B.J. (1996). *Co-opetition.* Currency Doubleday.

Breton, M., Pineault, R., Levesque, J.F., Roberge, D., Da Silva, R.B., Prud'homme, A. (2013). Reforming healthcare systems on a locally integrated basis: is there a potential for increasing collaborations in primary healthcare? *BMC Health Serv. Res, 13*(1), 262.
[http://dx.doi.org/10.1186/1472-6963-13-262] [PMID: 23835105]

Bruneo, H., Giacomini, E., Iannotta, G., Murthy, A., Patris, J. (2024). Risk and return in the biotech industry. *Int. J. Prod. Perform. Manag, 73*(6), 1926-1947.
[http://dx.doi.org/10.1108/IJPPM-04-2023-0179]

Brusoni, S., Prencipe, A., Pavitt, K. (2001). Knowledge specialization, organizational coupling, and the boundaries of the firm: Why do firms know more than they make? *Adm. Sci. Q, 46*(4), 597-621.
[http://dx.doi.org/10.2307/3094825]

Cabaleiro-Cerviño, G., Mendi, P. (2024). ESG-driven innovation strategy and firm performance. *Eurasian Business Review, 14*(1), 137-185.
[http://dx.doi.org/10.1007/s40821-024-00254-x]

Caroli, M. (2021). *Economia e gestione sostenibile delle imprese.* McGraw Hill Education.

Cassiman, B., Veugelers, R., Arts, S. (2018). Mind the gap: Capturing value from basic research through combining mobile inventors and partnerships. *Res. Policy, 47*(9), 1811-1824.
[http://dx.doi.org/10.1016/j.respol.2018.06.015]

Castañeda, D.I., Cuellar, S. (2020). Knowledge sharing and innovation: A systematic review. *Knowl. Process Manage, 27*(3), 159-173.
[http://dx.doi.org/10.1002/kpm.1637]

Castañer, X., Oliveira, N. (2020). Collaboration, coordination, and cooperation among organizations: Establishing the distinctive meanings of these terms through a systematic literature review. *J. Manage, 46*(6), 965-1001.
[http://dx.doi.org/10.1177/0149206320901565]

Cerved. (2022). *Rapporto Cerved PMI 2022.* Available from: https://www.cerved.com/ricerca--analisi/a/ricerca-analisi-imprese-mercati/rapporto-cerved-pmi-2022 [accessed 31 March 2026].

Chakkol, M., Selviaridis, K., Finne, M. (2018). The governance of collaboration in complex projects. *Int. J. Oper. Prod. Manage, 38*(4), 997-1019.
[http://dx.doi.org/10.1108/IJOPM-11-2017-0717]

Chalmers, L.M., Ashton, T., Tenbensel, T. (2017). Measuring and managing health system performance: An update from New Zealand. *Health Policy, 121*(8), 831-835.
[http://dx.doi.org/10.1016/j.healthpol.2017.05.012] [PMID: 28610840]

Chen, H., Engkvist, O., Wang, Y., Olivecrona, M., Blaschke, T. (2018). The rise of deep learning in drug discovery. *Drug Discov. Today, 23*(6), 1241-1250.
[http://dx.doi.org/10.1016/j.drudis.2018.01.039] [PMID: 29366762]

Chesbrough, H.W. (2003). *Open innovation: The new imperative for creating and profiting from technology.* Harvard Business School Press.

Chiaroni, D., Chiesa, V., Frattini, F. (2008). Patterns of collaboration along the bio-pharmaceutical innovation process. *Journal of Business Chemistry,* *5*(1), 7-22.

Çitilci, T., Akbalik, M. (2020). The importance of PESTEL analysis for environmental scanning process. In: Esen, Ö.A., Arslan, H., (Eds.), *Handbook of research on decision-making techniques in financial marketing* IGI Global.
[http://dx.doi.org/10.4018/978-1-7998-2559-3.ch016]

Clust-ER. (2025). *Clust-ER Health Emilia-Romagna.* Available from: https://www.art-er.it/clust-er [accessed 31 March 2026].

Cohen, W.M., Levinthal, D.A. (1990). Absorptive capacity: A new perspective on learning and innovation. *Adm. Sci. Q,* *35*(1), 128-152.
[http://dx.doi.org/10.2307/2393553]

DaSilva, E.J. (2004). The colours of biotechnology: Science, development and humankind. *Electron. J. Biotechnol,* *7*(3), 1-2.
[http://dx.doi.org/10.4067/S0717-34582004000300001]

de Gooyert, V., Rouwette, E., van Kranenburg, H., Freeman, E. (2017). Reviewing the role of stakeholders in Operational Research: A stakeholder theory perspective. *Eur. J. Oper. Res,* *262*(2), 402-410.
[http://dx.doi.org/10.1016/j.ejor.2017.03.079]

de Jong, M., Edelenbos, J., Teisman, G., Hoffman, J., Hajer, M. (2023). The explanatory power of the landscape perspective on inter-organizational collaboration. *Environ. Plann. A,* *55*(6), 1408-1427.
[http://dx.doi.org/10.1177/0308518X231152889]

de Wit-de Vries, E., Dolfsma, W.A., van der Windt, H.J., Gerkema, M.P. (2019). Knowledge transfer in university–industry research partnerships: a review. *J. Technol. Transf,* *44*(4), 1236-1255.
[http://dx.doi.org/10.1007/s10961-018-9660-x]

Delgado, M., Porter, M.E., Stern, S. (2014). Clusters, convergence, and economic performance. *Res. Policy,* *43*(10), 1785-1799.
[http://dx.doi.org/10.1016/j.respol.2014.05.007]

Deloitte. (2023). *Deciding on the right path: How biotechs should expand in(to) Europe.* Available from: https://www2.deloitte.com/uk/en/insights/industry/life-sciences/expanding-into-european-bio-ech-industry.html [accessed 31 March 2026].

DiMasi, J.A., Grabowski, H.G., Hansen, R.W. (2016). Innovation in the pharmaceutical industry: New estimates of R&D costs. *J. Health Econ,* *47*, 20-33.
[http://dx.doi.org/10.1016/j.jhealeco.2016.01.012] [PMID: 26928437]

Doz, Y.L. (2023). *In search of metanationals (INSEAD Working Paper No. 2023/14/STR).*
[http://dx.doi.org/10.2139/ssrn.4417190]

Doz, Y., Santos, J., Williamson, P. (2001). *From global to metanational: How companies win in the knowledge economy.* Harvard Business School Press.
[http://dx.doi.org/10.1145/503351.503119]

Dullaert, W., Ghiami, Y., Jagtenberg, C.J., Romero-Silva, R., Wissink, P.L.J., Zsidisin, G.A. (2025). An investigation of Dutch pharmaceutical supply chains: insights from the theory of swift and even flow. *Int. J. Logist. Manag,* *36*(7), 262-283.
[http://dx.doi.org/10.1108/IJLM-04-2024-0266]

Enginoğlu, D., Arikan, C.L. (2016). A literature review on core competencies. *Int. J. Manag,* *7*(3), 120-127.

[IJM].

Ernst & Young (EY) & Assobiotec–Federchimica. (2025). Il futuro di competenze e professioni nel biotech. *Ernst & Young.* Available from: https://assobiotec.federchimica.it/dati-e-analisi/biotecnologie [accessed 31 March 2026].

Ernst & Young (EY). (2023). *Beyond borders 2023: Biotech is facing a complex path forward.* Available from: https://www.ey.com/en_us/newsroom/2023/06/beyond-borders-2023-biotech-is-facing-a--omplex-path-forward-says-ey-report [accessed 31 March 2026].

Escher, I., Brzustewicz, P. (2020). Interorganizational collaboration on projects supporting sustainable development goals: The company perspective. *Sustainability (Basel), 12*(12), 4969. [http://dx.doi.org/10.3390/su12124969]

Esfandyarpour, A., Arasti, M.R., Farazi, M.S., Miremadi, I. (2024). From depth and breadth of knowledge to technological capability: a journey inside a firm's intellectual capital. *R & D Manag, 54*(4), 864-881. [http://dx.doi.org/10.1111/radm.12669]

Etit, D., Meramo, S., Ögmundarson, Ó., Jensen, M.K., Sukumara, S. (2024). Can biotechnology lead the way toward a sustainable pharmaceutical industry? *Curr. Opin. Biotechnol, 87*, 103100. [http://dx.doi.org/10.1016/j.copbio.2024.103100] [PMID: 38471403]

Etzkowitz, H., Leydesdorff, L. (2000). The dynamics of innovation: from National Systems and "Mode 2" to a Triple Helix of university–industry–government relations. *Res. Policy, 29*(2), 109-123. [http://dx.doi.org/10.1016/S0048-7333(99)00055-4]

Eudaric, A., Pellegrin, J-N. (2026). *The thriving biopharma business: How to unlock value and drive success in biotech and pharma.* Routledge.

EuropaBio. (2021). *EU industrial strategy 2020: EuropaBio welcomes increased focus on competitiveness and resilience driven by innovation and advanced technologies.* Available from: https://www.europabio.org/eu-industrial-strategy-2020-europabio-welcomes-increased-focus-on-compet-tiveness-and-resilience-driven-by-innovation-and-advanced-technologies/ [accessed 31 March 2026].

European Biotechnology Network. (2025). *About us.* Available from: https://european-biotechnology.net/about/ [accessed 31 March 2026].

European Commission. (2002). *Life sciences and biotechnology: A strategy for Europe (COM(2002)27).* Available from: https://ec.europa.eu/biotechnology/pdf/com2002-27_en.pdf [accessed 31 March 2026].

European Commission. (2019). *The European Green Deal: Striving to be the first climate-neutral continent.* Available from: https://commission.europa.eu/strategy-and-policy/priorities-2019-2024/european-green-deal_en [accessed 31 March 2026].

European Commission. (2020a). *EU4Health programme 2021–2027: A vision for a healthier European Union.* Available from: https://health.ec.europa.eu/funding/eu4health-programme-2021-2027-vi-ion-healthier-european-union_en [accessed 31 March 2026].

European Commission. (2020n). *Horizon Europe.* Available from: https://research-and-innovation.ec.europa.eu/funding/funding-opportunities/funding-programmes-and-open-calls/horizon-europe_en [accessed 31 March 2026].

European Commission. (2020c). *The Digital Europe Programme.* Available from: https://digital-strategy.ec.europa.eu/en/activities/digital-programme [accessed 31 March 2026].

European Commission. (2025a). *EU Industrial R&D Investment Scoreboard.* Available from: https://iri.jrc.ec.europa.eu/data [accessed 31 March 2026].

European Commission. (2025b). *Choosing Europe for life sciences: A strategy to make the EU the world's most sought-after place for life sciences by 2030 (COM(2025)525).* Available from: https://eur-lex.europa.eu/legal-content/IT/TXT/PDF/?uri=CELEX:52025DC0525 [accessed 31 March 2026].

European Environment Agency. (2025). *Europe's environment 2025.* Available from: https://www.eea.europa.eu/en/europe-environment-2025 [accessed 31 March 2026].

Eurostat. (2023). *EU investment in R&D increased to €331 billion in 2021.* Available from: https://ec.europa.eu/eurostat/web/products-eurostat-news/-/ddn-20231004-2 [accessed 31 March 2026].

Finegold, D., Frenkel, S. (2006). Managing people where people *really* matter: the management of human resources in biotech companies. *Int. J. Hum. Resour. Manage, 17*(1), 1-24.
[http://dx.doi.org/10.1080/09585190500366169]

Folta, T.B. (1998). Governance and uncertainty: the trade-off between administrative control and commitment. *Strateg. Manage. J, 19*(11), 1007-1028.
[http://dx.doi.org/10.1002/(SICI)1097-0266(199811O)19:11<1007::AID-SMJ999>3.0.CO;2-8]

Fontana, F., Caroli, M. (2013). *Economia e gestione delle imprese* McGraw-Hill.

Fraterman, S., Wübbels, G., Kniss, A. (2023). *The biotech opportunity in Europe.* Boston Consulting Group.

Freeman, R.E., Harrison, J.S., Wicks, A.C. (2007). *Managing for stakeholders: Survival, reputation, and success.* Yale University Press.

Freire, A., Gonçalves, P. (2022). Collaborative knowledge creation for sustainability-oriented innovation. *J. Knowl. Manage, 26*(5), 1007-1028.
[http://dx.doi.org/10.1108/JKM-09-2021-0710]

Giesecke, S. (2000). The contrasting roles of government in the development of biotechnology industry in the US and Germany. *Res. Policy, 29*(2), 205-223.
[http://dx.doi.org/10.1016/S0048-7333(99)00061-X]

GlaxoSmithKline (GSK). (2025). *Behind the science.* Available from: https://www.gsk.com/en-gb/ [accessed 31 March 2026].

Global Market Insights. (2021). *Biotechnology market – By application (Biopharmacy, Bioindustries, Bioservices, Bioagriculture, Bioinformatics), by technology (Fermentation, Tissue engineering and regeneration, PCR technology, Nanobiotechnology, Chromatography) & forecast, 2021–2027.* Available from: https://www.gminsights.com/industry-analysis/biotechnology-market [accessed 31 March 2026].

González-Sánchez, R., Alonso-Muñoz, S., Kocollari, U. (2025). Exploring the supply chain's transformation to achieve the sustainable development goals in the post-pandemic scenario: a review and a research agenda. *Int. J. Logist. Manag, 36*(7), 137-177.
[http://dx.doi.org/10.1108/IJLM-05-2023-0221]

Gottlieb, M.S., Schanker, H.M., Fan, P.T., Saxon, A., Weisman, J.D., Pozalski, I. (1981). Pneumocystis pneumonia--Los Angeles. *MMWR Morb. Mortal. Wkly. Rep, 30*(21), 250-252.
[PMID: 6265753]

Granstrand, O., Holgersson, M. (2020). Innovation ecosystems: A conceptual review and a new definition.

Technovation, 90-91, 102098.
[http://dx.doi.org/10.1016/j.technovation.2019.102098]

Grant, R.M. (2002). The knowledge-based view of the firm. In: Choo, C.W., Bontis, N., (Eds.), *The strategic management of intellectual capital and organizational knowledge* Oxford University Press.
[http://dx.doi.org/10.1093/oso/9780195138665.003.0008]

Grant, R.M. (2020). *Contemporary strategy analysis* Wiley.

Grant, R., Phene, A. (2022). The knowledge based view and global strategy: Past impact and future potential. *Glob. Strategy J, 12*(1), 3-30.
[http://dx.doi.org/10.1002/gsj.1399]

Grebe, S., Jarchow, S. (2025). "The dynamics of IP contract patterns in the German biotechnology industry – a mixed-methods approach". *J. Bus. Econ, 95*(1), 75-102.
[http://dx.doi.org/10.1007/s11573-024-01217-4]

Grupp, R.W., Gaines-Ross, L. (2002). Reputation management in the biotechnology industry. *J. Commer. Biotechnol, 9*(1), 17-26.
[http://dx.doi.org/10.1057/palgrave.jcb.3040003]

Gucciardi, G. (2024). Do venture capital investments contribute to the achievement of the sustainable development goals? *Bus. Strategy Environ, 33*(8), 8716-8746.
[http://dx.doi.org/10.1002/bse.3942]

Gulati, R., Wohlgezogen, F., Zhelyazkov, P. (2012). The two facets of collaboration: Cooperation and coordination in strategic alliances. *Acad. Management Ann, 6*(1), 531-583.
[http://dx.doi.org/10.5465/19416520.2012.691646]

Helfat, C.E., Martin, J.A. (2015). Dynamic managerial capabilities: Review and assessment of managerial impact on strategic change. *J. Manage, 41*(5), 1281-1312.
[http://dx.doi.org/10.1177/0149206314561301]

Henderson, R.M., Clark, K.B. (1990). Architectural innovation: The reconfiguration of existing product technologies and the failure of established firms. *Adm. Sci. Q, 35*(1), 9-30.
[http://dx.doi.org/10.2307/2393549]

Hermans, S., Sevenants, A., Declercq, A., Van Broeck, N., Deliens, L., Cohen, J., Van Audenhove, C. (2019). Integrated palliative care for nursing home residents: Exploring the challenges in the collaboration between nursing homes, home care and hospitals. *Int. J. Integr. Care, 19*(2), 3.
[http://dx.doi.org/10.5334/ijic.4186] [PMID: 30971869]

Hetemi, E., Ordieres, J., Nuur, C. (2022). Inter-organisational collaboration and knowledge-work: a contingency framework and evidence from a megaproject in Spain. *Knowl. Manag. Res. Pract, 20*(4), 641-653.
[http://dx.doi.org/10.1080/14778238.2022.2027827]

Hickey, G.M., Snyder, H.T., deVries, J.R., Temby, O. (2021). On inter-organizational trust, control and risk in transboundary fisheries governance. *Mar. Policy, 134*, 104772.
[http://dx.doi.org/10.1016/j.marpol.2021.104772]

Hietala, H., Päivärinta, T., Annanperä, E., Taskinen, P., Liukkunen, K. (2023). Toward collective ambidexterity in public sector digital initiatives: A case of the Finnish water sector. *Digital Government: Research and Practice, 4*(4), 1-23.

[http://dx.doi.org/10.1145/3609802]

Ho, J.K.K. (2014). Formulation of a systemic PEST analysis for strategic analysis. *Eur. Acad. Res, 2*(5), 6478-6492.

Hofer, C.W., Schendel, D. (1978). *Strategy formulation: Analytical concepts.* West Publishing.

Hofer, M.P., Criscuolo, P., Shah, N., Wal, A.L.J., Barlow, J. (2022). Regulatory policy and pharmaceutical innovation in the United Kingdom after Brexit: Initial insights. *Front. Med. (Lausanne), 9*, 1011082. [http://dx.doi.org/10.3389/fmed.2022.1011082] [PMID: 36590956]

Hunt, S.D., Hansen, J.M. (2010). The philosophical foundations of marketing research: For scientific realism and truth. In: Maclaran, P., Saren, M., Stern, B., Tadajewski, M., (Eds.), *The SAGE handbook of marketing theory* Sage Publications.
[http://dx.doi.org/10.4135/9781446222454.n7]

IBISBA – Industrial Biotechnology Innovation and Synthetic Biology Accelerator. (2025). *IBISBA research infrastructure for industrial biotechnology.* Available from: https://ibisba.eu [accessed 31 March 2026].

IBISWorld. (2025). *Global biotechnology industry report.* Available from: https://www.ibisworld.com/global/industry/global-biotechnology/ [accessed 31 March 2026].

International Council of Biotechnology Associations. (2023). *Biotechnology: Driving solutions for sustainable development.* Available from: https://go.bio.org/rs/490-EHZ-999/images/SDG%2C%20BIO%2C%20Report_2023.12.11.pdf [accessed 31 March 2026].

International Trade Administration. (2024). *Italy – Biotechnology.* Available from: https://www.trade.gov/country-commercial-guides/italy-biotechnology [accessed 31 March 2026].

IQS School of Management. (2023). *Competitiveness in biotechnology conference.* Available from: https://iqs.edu/en/iqs/news/competitiveness-biotechnology-conference/ [accessed 31 March 2026].

Jain, A. (2023). How knowledge loss and network-structure jointly determine R&D productivity in the biotechnology industry. *Technovation, 119*, 102607.
[http://dx.doi.org/10.1016/j.technovation.2022.102607]

Johnson, G., Whittington, R., Scholes, K. (2014). *Exploring strategy.* Pearson.

Júnior, L.C.R., Frederico, G.F., Costa, M.L.N. (2019). Supply chain management maturity and complexity: findings from a case study at a health biotechnology company in Brazil. *International Journal of Logistics Systems and Management, 33*(1), 99658.
[http://dx.doi.org/10.1504/IJLSM.2019.099658]

Junkunc, M.T. (2007). Managing radical innovation: The importance of specialized knowledge in the biotech revolution. *J. Bus. Venturing, 22*(3), 388-411.
[http://dx.doi.org/10.1016/j.jbusvent.2006.04.004]

Kafarski, P. (2012). Rainbow code of biotechnology. *Chemik, 66*(8), 811-816.

Kang, K.N., Park, H. (2012). Influence of government R&D support and inter-firm collaborations on innovation in Korean biotechnology SMEs. *Technovation, 32*(1), 68-78.
[http://dx.doi.org/10.1016/j.technovation.2011.08.004]

Khilji, S.E., Mroczkowski, T., Bernstein, B. (2006). From invention to innovation: Toward developing an integrated innovation model for biotech firms. *J. Prod. Innov. Manage, 23*(6), 528-540.

[http://dx.doi.org/10.1111/j.1540-5885.2006.00222.x]

Kim, R. (2019). *Economics and management in the biopharmaceutical industry in the USA: Evolution and strategic change.* Routledge.

King, A. (2025). *Four ways to power-up AI for drug discovery.* Nature Outlook.
[http://dx.doi.org/10.1038/d41586-025-00602-5]

Kourti, I. (2021). Managing the identity paradox in inter□organisational collaborations. *Eur. Manag. Rev, 18*(4), 445-459.
[http://dx.doi.org/10.1111/emre.12485]

Kremer, H., Villamor, I., Aguinis, H. (2019). Innovation leadership: Best-practice recommendations for promoting employee creativity, voice, and knowledge sharing. *Bus. Horiz, 62*(1), 65-74.
[http://dx.doi.org/10.1016/j.bushor.2018.08.010]

Kretschmer, T., Vanneste, B.S. (2017). Collaboration in strategic alliances: Cooperation and coordination. In: Mesquita, L.F., Reuer, J.J., Ragozzino, R., (Eds.), *Collaborative strategy: Critical issues for alliances and networks* Edward Elgar.
[http://dx.doi.org/10.4337/9781783479580.00015]

Labiotech. (2023a). *AELIX announces important step towards HIV eradication.* Available from: https://www.labiotech.eu/trends-news/aelix-therapeutics-important-step-hiv-eradication/ [accessed 31 March 2026].

Labiotech. (2023b). *Fourteen biotech companies with market caps exceeding $100 billion.* Available from: https://www.labiotech.eu/best-biotech/biotech-companies-highest-market-cap/ [accessed 31 March 2026].

Lavikka, R., Smeds, R., Jaatinen, M. (2015). A process for building inter-organizational contextual ambidexterity. *Bus. Process. Manag. J, 21*(5), 1140-1161.
[http://dx.doi.org/10.1108/BPMJ-12-2013-0153]

Le Pennec, M., Raufflet, E. (2018). Value creation in inter-organizational collaboration: An empirical study. *J. Bus. Ethics, 148*(4), 817-834.
[http://dx.doi.org/10.1007/s10551-015-3012-7]

Leiponen, A.E. (2008). Competing through cooperation: The organization of standard setting in wireless telecommunications. *Manage. Sci, 54*(11), 1904-1919.
[http://dx.doi.org/10.1287/mnsc.1080.0912]

Lin, M., Lekhawipat, W. (2023). Key influencing factors for the success of external innovation strategies in the biotechnology industry. *J. Bus. Ind. Mark, 38*(12), 2745-2759.
[http://dx.doi.org/10.1108/JBIM-07-2022-0307]

Liu, Z., Ding, R. (2023). Dynamic evaluation of project governance in collaborative innovation projects: A case of industry technology research institute. *Sustainability (Basel), 15*(16), 12493.
[http://dx.doi.org/10.3390/su151612493]

Lowe, M.M., Blaser, D.A., Cone, L., Arcona, S., Ko, J., Sasane, R., Wicks, P. (2016). Increasing patient involvement in drug development. *Value Health, 19*(6), 869-878.
[http://dx.doi.org/10.1016/j.jval.2016.04.009] [PMID: 27712716]

Mak, K.K., Pichika, M.R. (2019). Artificial intelligence in drug development: present status and future prospects. *Drug Discov. Today, 24*(3), 773-780.

[http://dx.doi.org/10.1016/j.drudis.2018.11.014] [PMID: 30472429]

Mardani, A., Nikoosokhan, S., Moradi, M., Doustar, M. (2018). The relationship between knowledge management and innovation performance. *J. High Technol. Manage. Res, 29*(1), 12-26.
[http://dx.doi.org/10.1016/j.hitech.2018.04.002]

McGlinchey, Y., Iqbal, J., Trubetskaya, A., Thenarasu, M., McDermott, O. (2025). Design for green lean six sigma to improve sustainability in the pharmaceutical industry – a case study. *Prod. Manuf. Res, 13*(1), 2461010.
[http://dx.doi.org/10.1080/21693277.2025.2461010]

McKenzie, K., Smith-Merry, J. (2023). Responding to Complexity in the Context of the National Disability Insurance Scheme. *Soc. Policy Soc, 22*(1), 139-154.
[http://dx.doi.org/10.1017/S1474746422000562]

McKinsey & Company. (2019). *Biotech in Europe: A strong foundation for growth and innovation.* Available from: https://www.mckinsey.com/~/media/McKinsey/Industries/Pharmaceuticals%20and%20Medical%20Products/Our%20Insights/Biotech%20in%20Europe%20A%20strong%20foundation%20for%20growth%20and%20innovation/Biotech-in-Europe-A-strong-foundation-for-growth-and-innovation.pdf [accessed 31 March 2026].

McKinsey & Company. (2021). *Can European biotechs achieve greater scale in a fragmented landscape?.* Available from: https://www.mckinsey.com/industries/life-sciences/our-insights/can-european-biotchs-achieve-greater-scale-in-a-fragmented-landscape [accessed 31 March 2026].

McMillan, G.S., Hamilton, R.D., III, Deeds, D.L. (2000). Firm management of scientific information: an empirical update. *R & D Manag, 30*(2), 177-182.
[http://dx.doi.org/10.1111/1467-9310.00167]

Mervyn, K., Amoo, N., Malby, R. (2019). Challenges and insights in inter-organizational collaborative healthcare networks. *Int. J. Organ. Anal, 27*(4), 875-902.
[http://dx.doi.org/10.1108/IJOA-05-2018-1415]

Miller, D., Friesen, P.H. (1983). Strategy□making and environment: The third link. *Strateg. Manage. J, 4*(3), 221-235.
[http://dx.doi.org/10.1002/smj.4250040304]

Mintzberg, H. (1983). *Structure in fives: Designing effective organizations.* Prentice-Hall.

Mintzberg, H. (1994). The fall and rise of strategic planning. *Harv. Bus. Rev, 72*(1), 107-114.

Mintzberg, H. (2017). Crafting strategy. In: Berends, E., Bakker, G.D., van Aken, J.A.E., (Eds.), *The aesthetic turn in management* Routledge.
[http://dx.doi.org/10.4324/9781351147965-23]

Mitze, T., Strotebeck, F. (2019). Determining factors of interregional research collaboration in Germany's biotech network: Capacity, proximity, policy? *Technovation, 80-81*, 40-53.
[http://dx.doi.org/10.1016/j.technovation.2018.11.001]

Molloy, P.L., Johnson, L.W. (2016). Biotechnology, a strategic planning orphan: towards an effective strategy framework for biotechnology firms. *J. Commer. Biotechnol, 22*(3), 118-125.
[http://dx.doi.org/10.5912/jcb748]

Moradi, M., Dass, M. (2022). Applications of artificial intelligence in B2B marketing: Challenges and future directions. *Ind. Mark. Manage, 107*, 300-314.

[http://dx.doi.org/10.1016/j.indmarman.2022.10.016]

Mowery, D.C., Oxley, J.E., Silverman, B.S. (1996). Strategic alliances and interfirm knowledge transfer. *Strateg. Manage. J, 17*(S2), 77-91.
[http://dx.doi.org/10.1002/smj.4250171108]

Najafi-Tavani, S., Naudé, P., Smith, P., Khademi-Gerashi, M. (2023). Teach well, learn better - Customer involvement and new product performance in B2B markets: The role of desorptive and absorptive capacity. *Ind. Mark. Manage, 108*, 263-275.
[http://dx.doi.org/10.1016/j.indmarman.2022.12.001]

Nguyen, G., Turner, M. (2023). BIA UK biotech financing 2023. *BioIndustry Association.* Available from: https://biotechfinance.org/wp-content/uploads/2024/01/BIA-Finance-report-26-01-24.pdf [accessed 31 March 2026].

Nguyen, P.T.M., Mai, K.N., Nguyen, P.N.D. (2023). Does trust affect inter-organizational governance mechanisms and collaboration via innovation? *Sustainability, 15*(12), 9547.
[http://dx.doi.org/10.3390/su15129547]

Nickerson, J.A., Zenger, T.R. (2004). A knowledge-based theory of the firm: The problem-solving perspective. *Organ. Sci, 15*(6), 617-632.
[http://dx.doi.org/10.1287/orsc.1040.0093]

Niosi, J., McKelvey, M. (2018). Relating business model innovations and innovation cascades: the case of biotechnology. *J. Evol. Econ, 28*(5), 1081-1109.
[http://dx.doi.org/10.1007/s00191-018-0561-9] [PMID: 30613125]

Nippa, M., Reuer, J.J. (2019). On the future of international joint venture research. *J. Int. Bus. Stud, 50*(4), 555-597.
[http://dx.doi.org/10.1057/s41267-019-00212-0]

Nonaka, I., Takeuchi, H., Umemoto, K. (1996). A theory of organizational knowledge creation. *Int. J. Technol. Manag, 11*(7–8), 833-845.
[http://dx.doi.org/10.1504/IJTM.1996.025472]

O'Reilly, C.A., III, Tushman, M.L. (2013). Organizational ambidexterity: Past, present, and future. *Acad. Manage. Perspect, 27*(4), 324-338.
[http://dx.doi.org/10.5465/amp.2013.0025]

Office for Life Sciences. (2017). *Life sciences industrial strategy.* Available from: https://assets.publishing.service.gov.uk/media/5a74aeaced915d7ab83b5b0b/LifeSciencesIndustrialStrategy_acc2.pdf [accessed 31 March 2026].

Oliveira, N., Lumineau, F., Ariño, A. (2023). Time in international strategic alliances: Progress and prospect. *J. World Bus, 58*(4), 101456.
[http://dx.doi.org/10.1016/j.jwb.2023.101456]

Olk, P., West, J. (2020). The relationship of industry structure to open innovation: cooperative value creation in pharmaceutical consortia. *R & D Manag, 50*(1), 116-135.
[http://dx.doi.org/10.1111/radm.12364]

Onetti, A., Zucchella, A. (2014). *Business modeling for life science and biotech companies: Creating value and competitive advantage with the milestone bridge.* Routledge.
[http://dx.doi.org/10.4324/9781315852584]

Organisation for Economic Co-operation and Development (OECD) & European Commission. (2024). *Health at a glance: Europe 2024*, OECD Publishing.
[http://dx.doi.org/10.1787/b3704e14-en]

Organisation for Economic Co-operation and Development (OECD). (2005). *A framework for biotechnology statistics.* Available from: https://one.oecd.org/document/DSTI/EAS/STP/NESTI(2005)8/FINAL/en/pdf [accessed 31 March 2026].

Osservatorio Malattie Rare (OMAR). (2025). *Nasce Xellbiogene: joint venture tra Bambino Gesù e Gemelli per la sperimentazione nel campo delle biotecnologie.* Available from: https://www.osservatoriomalattierare.it/news/attualita/5537-nasce-xellbiogene-joint-venture-tra-bambino-gesu-e-gmelli-per-la-sperimentazione-nel-campo-delle-biotecnologie [accessed 31 March 2026].

Osterwalder, A., Pigneur, Y. (2010). *Business model generation.* John Wiley & Sons.

Otte-Trojel, T., Rundall, T.G., de Bont, A., van de Klundert, J. (2017). Relational coordination in interorganizational networks. *Int. J. Healthc. Manag,* *10*(2), 75-83.
[http://dx.doi.org/10.1080/20479700.2015.1101911]

Owen-Smith, J., Powell, W.W. (2004). Knowledge networks and spillovers in biotechnology. *Organ. Sci,* *15*(1), 5-21.
[http://dx.doi.org/10.1287/orsc.1030.0054]

Palmatier, R.W., Crecelius, A.T. (2019). The "first principles" of marketing strategy. *AMS Rev,* *9*(1-2), 5-26.
[http://dx.doi.org/10.1007/s13162-019-00134-y]

Peng, Y., Liao, W. (2025). Inventory routing optimization for pharmaceutical cold chain logistics from economic and environmental perspective. *International Journal of Systems Science: Operations & Logistics,* *12*(1), 2474690.
[http://dx.doi.org/10.1080/23302674.2025.2474690]

Pfizer. (2025). *Pfizer and BioNTech announce further details of collaboration.* Available from: https://www.pfizer.com/news/press-release/press-release-detail/pfizer-and-biontech-anounce-further-details-collaboration [accessed 31 March 2026].

Pharma Boardroom. (2022). *Ten Spanish biotechs to watch in 2022.* Available from: https://pharmaboardroom.com/articles/ten-spanish-biotechs-to-watch-in-2022/ [accessed 31 March 2026].

Philippidis, A. (2024). Top 25 biotech companies of 2024. *Genet. Eng. Biotechnol. News,* *44*(1), 22-23.
[http://dx.doi.org/10.1089/gen.44.01.07]

Pires, R.A.R., Ferreira, J.J. (2025). Bridging innovation strategies and intellectual property: A systematic review-based conceptual framework and a roadmap for future research. *Technovation,* *144*, 103243.
[http://dx.doi.org/10.1016/j.technovation.2025.103243]

Pisano, G.P. (2006). *Science business.* Harvard Business Press.

Porter, M.E. (1985). *Competitive advantage: Creating and sustaining superior performance.* Free Press.

Porter, M.E. (1989). How competitive forces shape strategy. In: Asch, D., Bowman, C., (Eds.), *Readings in strategic management* Macmillan.
[http://dx.doi.org/10.1007/978-1-349-20317-8_10]

Porter, M.E. (2008). The five competitive forces that shape strategy. *Harv. Bus. Rev,* *86*(1), 78-93, 137.

[PMID: 18271320]

Porter, M.E., Kramer, M.R. (2019). Creating shared value. In: Lenssen, G.G., Smith, N.C., (Eds.), *Managing sustainable business* Springer Nature.
[http://dx.doi.org/10.1007/978-94-024-1144-7_16]

Porumboiu, C. (2020). The importance of emerging industries: The case of biopharma. In: Bilgin, M.H., (Ed.), *Eurasian economic perspectives* Springer.
[http://dx.doi.org/10.1007/978-3-030-48531-3_1]

Powell, W.W. (1996). Inter-organizational collaboration in the biotechnology industry. *J. Inst. Theor. Econ, 152*(1), 197-215.

Powell, W.W., Koput, K.W., Smith-Doerr, L. (1996). Interorganizational collaboration and the locus of innovation: Networks of learning in biotechnology. *Adm. Sci. Q, 41*(1), 116-145.
[http://dx.doi.org/10.2307/2393988]

Powell, W.W., White, D.R., Koput, K.W., Owen-Smith, J. (2005). Network dynamics and field evolution. *Am. J. Sociol, 110*(4), 1132-1205.
[http://dx.doi.org/10.1086/421508]

Prahalad, C.K., Hamel, G. (1999). The core competence of the corporation. In: Zack, C., (Ed.), *Knowledge and strategy* Routledge.
[http://dx.doi.org/10.1016/B978-0-7506-7088-3.50006-1]

PricewaterhouseCoopers LLP. (2025). *UK Life Sciences Future50: Momentum in an evolving landscape.* Available from: https://www.pwc.co.uk/industries/assets/life-sciences-future50.pdf [accessed 31 March 2026].

Quintana-García, C., Benavides-Velasco, C.A. (2004). Cooperation, competition, and innovative capability: a panel data of European dedicated biotechnology firms. *Technovation, 24*(12), 927-938.
[http://dx.doi.org/10.1016/S0166-4972(03)00060-9]

Radaelli, G., Spyridonidis, D., Currie, G. (2024). Platform evolution in large INTER□ORGANIZATIONAL collaborative research programs. *J. Oper. Manage, 70*(1), 22-49.
[http://dx.doi.org/10.1002/joom.1273]

Roehrich, J.K., Selviaridis, K., Kalra, J., Van der Valk, W., Fang, F. (2020). Inter-organizational governance: a review, conceptualisation and extension. *Prod. Plann. Contr, 31*(6), 453-469.
[http://dx.doi.org/10.1080/09537287.2019.1647364]

Rybnicek, R., Königsgruber, R. (2019). Industry–university collaboration success factors. *J. Bus. Econ, 89*(2), 221-250.
[http://dx.doi.org/10.1007/s11573-018-0916-6]

Schepman, S., Valentijn, P., Bruijnzeels, M., Maaijen, M., de Bakker, D., Batenburg, R., de Bont, A. (2018). Do project management and network governance contribute to inter-organisational collaboration in primary care? A mixed methods study. *BMC Health Serv. Res, 18*(1), 427.
[http://dx.doi.org/10.1186/s12913-018-3169-8] [PMID: 29879971]

Schneider, P., Walters, W.P., Plowright, A.T., Sieroka, N., Listgarten, J., Goodnow, R.A., Jr, Fisher, J., Jansen, J.M., Duca, J.S., Rush, T.S., Zentgraf, M., Hill, J.E., Krutoholow, E. (2020). Rethinking drug design in the artificial intelligence era. *Nat. Rev. Drug Discov, 19*(5), 353-364.
[http://dx.doi.org/10.1038/s41573-019-0050-3] [PMID: 31801986]

Seidl, D., Werle, F. (2018). Inter□organizational sensemaking in the face of strategic meta□problems: Requisite variety and dynamics of participation. *Strateg. Manage. J, 39*(3), 830-858.
[http://dx.doi.org/10.1002/smj.2723]

Shafer, S.M., Smith, H.J., Linder, J.C. (2005). The power of business models. *Bus. Horiz, 48*(3), 199-207.
[http://dx.doi.org/10.1016/j.bushor.2004.10.014]

Sharma, A., Pathak, S., Borah, S.B., Adhikary, A. (2022). Collaboration strategies in buyer-supplier relational (BSR) networks and sustainable firm performance: A trade-off story. *Int. J. Prod. Econ, 253*, 108558.
[http://dx.doi.org/10.1016/j.ijpe.2022.108558]

Sheth, J.N., Parvatiyar, A. (2021). Sustainable marketing: Market-driving, not market-driven. *J. Macromark, 41*(1), 150-165.
[http://dx.doi.org/10.1177/0276146720961836]

Shimasaki, C. (2020). Biotechnology products and their customers: Developing a successful market strategy. In: Shimasaki, C., (Ed.), *Biotechnology entrepreneurship* Academic Press.
[http://dx.doi.org/10.1016/B978-0-12-815585-1.00032-2]

Shimasaki, C.D. (2008). *The business of bioscience.* Springer.

Shimasaki, C.D. (2014). *Biotechnology entrepreneurship: Starting, managing, and leading biotech companies.* Academic Press.
[http://dx.doi.org/10.1016/B978-0-12-404730-3.00004-X]

Shipilov, A., Gawer, A. (2020). Integrating research on inter-organizational networks and ecosystems. *Acad. Management Ann, 14*(1), 92-121.
[http://dx.doi.org/10.5465/annals.2018.0121]

Silva, E. M., Paiva, E. L., Sacomano Neto, M., Freitas, K. A. D. (2021). Developing operational capabilities in the collaborative practice-adoption process through different triadic structures. *Brazilian Administration Review, 18*, e210025.

Simon, F., Giovannetti, G. (2017). *Managing biotechnology: From science to market in the digital age.* Wiley.

Skare, M., Gavurova, B., Rigelsky, M. (2023). Innovation activity and the outcomes of B2C, B2B, and B2G E-Commerce in EU countries. *J. Bus. Res, 163*, 113874.
[http://dx.doi.org/10.1016/j.jbusres.2023.113874]

Skvarka, J., Farkas, C. (2013). Building a fully integrated biotech company: What it takes. *In Vivo: The Business &. Med-Rep,* (September), 1-8. Available from: https://media.bain.com/Images/IN_VIVO_Building_a_fully_integrated_biotech_company.pdf [accessed 31 March 2026].

Smith, M., Sarabi, Y., Christopoulos, D. (2023). Understanding collaboration patterns on funded research projects: A network analysis. *Netw. Sci, 11*(1), 143-173.
[http://dx.doi.org/10.1017/nws.2022.33]

Sobrero, M., Roberts, E.B. (2002). Strategic management of supplier–manufacturer relations in new product development. *Res. Policy, 31*(1), 159-182.
[http://dx.doi.org/10.1016/S0048-7333(00)00157-8]

Sorrentino, F., Garraffo, F. (2012). Explaining performing R&D through alliances: Implications for the business model of Italian dedicated biotech firms. *J. Manag. Gov, 16*(3), 449-475.

[http://dx.doi.org/10.1007/s10997-010-9159-9]

Statista. (2024a). *Biotechnology industry – Statistics & facts.* Available from: https://www.statista.com/topics/1634/biotechnology-industry/ [accessed 31 March 2026].

Statista. (2024b). *Total number of biotechnology firms in selected European countries in 2022.* Available from: https://www.statista.com/statistics/439960/number-of-biotechnology-companies-europe-eu/ [accessed 31 March 2026].

Statista. (2025a). *Number of enterprises in biotechnology research and experimental development in the United Kingdom from 2008 to 2023.* Available from: https://www.statista.com/statistics/471435/biotechnology-research-and-development-enterprises-uk-united-kingdom/ [accessed 31 March 2026].

Statista. (2025b). *Number of biotechnology patents granted by the European Patent Office from 2014 to 2024.* Available from: https://www.statista.com/statistics/461706/number-patents-in-biotechnology-se-tor-european-union-eu/ [accessed 31 March 2026].

Steyer, V., Gilbert, C. (2013). Exploring the ambiguous consensus on public–private partnerships in collective risk preparation. *Sociol. Health Illn, 35*(2), 292-303.
[http://dx.doi.org/10.1111/j.1467-9566.2012.01538.x] [PMID: 23301727]

Szulanski, G. (1996). Exploring internal stickiness: Impediments to the transfer of best practice within the firm. *Strateg. Manage. J, 17*(S2), 27-43.
[http://dx.doi.org/10.1002/smj.4250171105]

Tallman, S., Jenkins, M., Henry, N., Pinch, S. (2004). Knowledge, clusters, and competitive advantage. *Acad. Manage. Rev, 29*(2), 258-271.
[http://dx.doi.org/10.5465/amr.2004.12736089]

Taylor, M., Doerfel, M.L. (2005). Another dimension to explicating relationships: measuring inter-organizational linkages. *Public Relat. Rev, 31*(1), 121-129.
[http://dx.doi.org/10.1016/j.pubrev.2004.11.013]

Tee, R., Davies, A., Whyte, J. (2019). Modular designs and integrating practices: Managing collaboration through coordination and cooperation. *Res. Policy, 48*(1), 51-61.
[http://dx.doi.org/10.1016/j.respol.2018.07.017]

Teece, D.J. (2007). Explicating dynamic capabilities: the nature and microfoundations of (sustainable) enterprise performance. *Strateg. Manage. J, 28*(13), 1319-1350.
[http://dx.doi.org/10.1002/smj.640]

Teece, D.J. (2018). Business models and dynamic capabilities. *Long Range Plann, 51*(1), 40-49.
[http://dx.doi.org/10.1016/j.lrp.2017.06.007]

Teece, D.J., Pisano, G., Shuen, A. (1997). Dynamic capabilities and strategic management. *Strateg. Manage. J, 18*(7), 509-533.
[http://dx.doi.org/10.1002/(SICI)1097-0266(199708)18:7<509::AID-SMJ882>3.0.CO;2-Z]

Topol, E.J. (2019). High-performance medicine: the convergence of human and artificial intelligence. *Nat. Med, 25*(1), 44-56.
[http://dx.doi.org/10.1038/s41591-018-0300-7] [PMID: 30617339]

Tran, L. (2023). Avid, Averse, Apprehensive, or Apathetic? A typology of collaboration attitudes. *Nonprofit Manag. Leadersh, 34*(1), 131-153.

[http://dx.doi.org/10.1002/nml.21565]

Trincado-Munoz, F., van Metteren, M., Rubin, T.H., Vorley, T. (2022). *Mapping the biotechnology and bioscience industry in the UK: A knowledge space analysis.* Available from: https://innovationcaucus.co.uk/app/uploads/2022/10/BIOSCIENCE2-Mapping-bioscience-industry.pdf [accessed 31 March 2026].

United Nations. (2015). *Transforming our world: The 2030 agenda for sustainable development.* Available from: https://sdgs.un.org/2030agenda [accessed 31 March 2026].

United Nations. (2025). *Sustainable development goals.* Available from: https://www.un.org/sustainabledevelopment/ [accessed 31 March 2026].

University of Urbino Carlo Bo. (2025). *EryDel: ricerca e impresa biotech.* Available from: https://uniamo.uniurb.it/erydel-ricerca-impresa-biotech/ [accessed 31 March 2026].

Vamathevan, J., Clark, D., Czodrowski, P., Dunham, I., Ferran, E., Lee, G., Li, B., Madabhushi, A., Shah, P., Spitzer, M., Zhao, S. (2019). Applications of machine learning in drug discovery and development. *Nat. Rev. Drug Discov, 18*(6), 463-477.
[http://dx.doi.org/10.1038/s41573-019-0024-5] [PMID: 30976107]

Vangen, S., Hayes, J.P., Cornforth, C. (2015). Governing cross-sector, inter-organizational collaborations. *Public Manage. Rev, 17*(9), 1237-1260.
[http://dx.doi.org/10.1080/14719037.2014.903658]

Varadarajan, R. (2010). Strategic marketing and marketing strategy: domain, definition, fundamental issues and foundational premises. *J. Acad. Mark. Sci, 38*(2), 119-140.
[http://dx.doi.org/10.1007/s11747-009-0176-7]

Vurro, C., Romito, S., Costanzo, L.A., Ghobadian, A., Russo, A. (2024). Alliance management capabilities in sustainability□oriented collaboration: Problematization and new research directions. *Int. J. Manag. Rev, 26*(1), 8-33.
[http://dx.doi.org/10.1111/ijmr.12346]

Wang, M., Jie, F. (2020). Managing supply chain uncertainty and risk in the pharmaceutical industry. *Health Serv. Manage. Res, 33*(3), 156-164.
[http://dx.doi.org/10.1177/0951484819845305] [PMID: 31213085]

Wang, S., Yang, L. (2022). The network structure of innovation networks. *Netw. Spat. Econ, 22*(1), 65-96.
[http://dx.doi.org/10.1007/s11067-021-09556-3]

Way, D., Bouder, F., Löfstedt, R., Evensen, D. (2016). Medicines transparency at the European Medicines Agency (EMA) in the new information age: the perspectives of patients. *J. Risk Res, 19*(9), 1185-1215.
[http://dx.doi.org/10.1080/13669877.2016.1200652]

WifOR Institute. (2020). *Measuring the economic footprint of the biotechnology industry in Europe.* Available from: https://www.wifor.com/uploads/2021/03/201215_WifOR_EuropaBIO_Economic_Impact_Biotech_FINAL.pdf [accessed 31 March 2026].

Wilson, G.A., York, J.M. (2023). Reducing risk and increasing performance in the biotechnology industry. *Journal of the International Council for Small Business, 4*(2), 184-195.
[http://dx.doi.org/10.1080/26437015.2022.2073297]

Windeler, A., Sydow, J. (2001). Project networks and changing industry practices. *Organ. Stud, 22*(6), 1035-1060.

[http://dx.doi.org/10.1177/0170840601226006]

Yang, J., Zhang, J., Zeng, D. (2022). Scientific collaboration networks and firm innovation: the contingent impact of a dynamic environment. *Manage. Decis, 60*(1), 278-296.
[http://dx.doi.org/10.1108/MD-08-2020-1050]

Yüksel, I. (2012). Developing a multi-criteria decision-making model for PESTEL analysis. *Int. J. Bus. Manage, 7*(24), 52-66.
[http://dx.doi.org/10.5539/ijbm.v7n24p52]

Zhavoronkov, A., Ivanenkov, Y.A., Aliper, A., Veselov, M.S., Aladinskiy, V.A., Aladinskaya, A.V., Terentiev, V.A., Polykovskiy, D.A., Kuznetsov, M.D., Asadulaev, A., Volkov, Y., Zholus, A., Shayakhmetov, R.R., Zhebrak, A., Minaeva, L.I., Zagribelnyy, B.A., Lee, L.H., Soll, R., Madge, D., Xing, L., Guo, T., Aspuru-Guzik, A., Vanhaelen, Q. (2019). Deep learning enables rapid identification of potent DDR1 kinase inhibitors. *Nat. Biotechnol, 37*(9), 1038-1040.
[http://dx.doi.org/10.1038/s41587-019-0224-x] [PMID: 31477924]

Zhou, J., Guo, A., Chen, Y., Chen, J. (2022). Original innovation through inter-organizational collaboration. *Sustainability (Basel), 14*(10), 6162.
[http://dx.doi.org/10.3390/su14106162]

Ziehe, D., Helfen, M. (2021). "You are not my boss!": Managing inter-organizational collaboration in German ground handling operations. *German Journal of Human Resource Management: Zeitschrift für Personalforschung, 35*(3), 356-382.
[http://dx.doi.org/10.1177/2397002220978114]

Zuzak, T.J., Boňková, J., Careddu, D., Garami, M., Hadjipanayis, A., Jazbec, J., Merrick, J., Miller, J., Ozturk, C., Persson, I.A.L., Petrova, G., Saz Peiró, P., Schraub, S., Simões-Wüst, A.P., Steinsbekk, A., Stockert, K., Stoimenova, A., Styczynski, J., Tzenova-Savova, A., Ventegodt, S., Vlieger, A.M., Längler, A. (2013). Use of complementary and alternative medicine by children in Europe: Published data and expert perspectives. *Complement. Ther. Med, 21* (Suppl. 1), S34-S47.
[http://dx.doi.org/10.1016/j.ctim.2012.01.001] [PMID: 23578916]

SUBJECT INDEX

A

Acquisitions 2, 29, 43, 44, 45, 46, 48, 49, 73, 74, 78
Activities, primary 4, 71, 72, 76, 78
Agencies, regulatory 23, 73, 75, 77, 80, 81, 82, 86
Agreements 24, 32, 41, 42
Agri-food 38, 41, 57
Agriculture 1, 16, 53, 58, 80, 81, 87
AI-enabled biotech firms 64, 66
Algorithms 73, 77
Alignment 33, 72, 78, 90
Alliances 30, 34, 39, 40, 51
Alliances, strategic 29, 30, 36, 44, 58, 80, 81, 86, 88
Amgen 14, 48, 49, 50, 85
Applications 3, 11, 18, 27, 42, 60
Aquaculture 4, 24

B

Balance 32, 33, 43, 51
Barriers 19, 30, 31, 33, 34, 43, 53, 56
Biobased Industries Consortium (BIC) 37
Bioinformatics 5, 49
Biological data 66, 68
Biomedical research 62, 65, 69, 90
BioNTech 15, 36, 67, 68
Biotech firms 4, 13, 18, 20, 23, 44, 46, 52, 53, 58, 60, 63, 66, 67, 76, 78
Biotechnology 5, 6, 7, 23, 24, 29, 30, 42, 53, 57, 65, 68, 70, 84, 89
Biotechnology processes 63, 64
Biotechnology products 41, 43, 56, 58
Business models 52, 53, 54, 55, 57, 58, 59, 60, 61, 63, 64, 67, 69, 70

C

Capabilities 31, 49, 64, 65, 73, 89
Capacity 18, 27, 36, 42, 56, 65, 68, 79, 88, 89, 90
Capital 30, 38, 42, 47, 51, 60
Challenges 22, 31, 38, 42, 43, 57, 58, 61, 88
Channels 54, 55, 60
Clinical data 62, 63, 76, 85
Clinical trials 27, 41, 56, 58, 60, 62, 63, 74, 75
Collaborations 20, 24, 26, 30, 31, 32, 33, 34, 35, 39, 40, 41, 51, 66, 69
Collaborative networks 31, 43, 52, 53, 58, 69, 87, 88, 89
Commercialization 36, 47, 58, 63, 69, 80, 89
Communication 34, 37, 64, 81, 89
Competencies 12, 33, 64, 65, 66, 70, 71, 76, 77, 78, 79
Competitiveness 12, 18, 21, 29, 30, 37, 39, 43, 50, 51, 84, 88
Complexity 21, 22, 34, 41, 42, 51, 58, 61, 69
Conditions 5, 6, 19, 29, 34, 44
Configurations 57, 58, 59, 63, 64, 66, 67, 68, 69
Coordination 31, 34, 35, 43, 61, 75, 77, 88
Costs 19, 32, 40, 52, 56, 58, 73, 74, 83
Cross-sector collaborations 29, 38, 39, 40, 41, 42, 43, 44

D

Dedicated Biotech Firms (DBFS) 4, 52, 57, 58, 59
Delivery 72, 74, 75, 78
Design 11, 18, 43, 52, 53, 63, 64, 67, 70
Development cycles 41, 43, 52, 53, 56, 69, 70, 71, 79, 88
Diagnostics 4, 58, 63
Digital technologies 7, 40, 43, 52, 64, 77
Dimensions 12, 34, 66, 88, 89
Discoveries 3, 25, 62, 63, 89
Distribution 3, 4, 16, 17, 21, 34, 41, 61, 71, 72, 78
Distribution channels 28, 30, 75
Domains 11, 50, 58, 64

Paola Olimpia Achard

Drugs 18, 21, 43
Dynamics 59, 70, 82

E

Ecosystems 36, 38, 56, 59, 89
Effectiveness 7, 31, 33, 34, 35, 42
Europe 3, 4, 5, 6, 7, 8, 9, 10, 11, 12, 13, 14, 18, 19, 20
European biotech firms 5, 27, 28, 30, 52
European Commission 2, 6, 7, 8, 9, 12, 37
Evolution 30, 63, 64, 67, 89, 90
Exchange 39, 42, 44, 51
Exit strategies 43, 44, 51, 76
Experimentation 60, 65, 66, 71, 73, 89
Expertise 21, 38, 39, 41, 42, 43, 46, 51, 52, 64, 85

F

Factors 5, 6, 8, 18, 19, 22, 27, 30, 31, 33, 34, 35, 44, 46
Financial resources 1, 44, 59, 69, 87
Firms 2, 3, 4, 5, 6, 13, 16, 18, 19, 20, 21, 22, 23, 31, 36, 53, 57, 58, 65, 88
Fully integrated firm (FIF) 57, 58, 59
Funding 24, 26, 37, 39, 57, 77
Funding, public 26, 58, 59, 60, 82

G

GDP (Gross Domestic Product) 9, 10, 24
Genomic data 64, 65, 68
Governance 34, 35, 74, 84, 86, 87
Governance mechanisms 29, 31, 32, 34, 35, 49, 86, 89
Growth 1, 2, 6, 9, 11, 13, 14, 16, 20, 25, 26, 27, 43

H

Health 4, 15, 28, 80, 84
Healthcare 1, 9, 11, 28, 31, 37, 53, 56, 57, 81, 87
Healthcare institutions 33, 86, 89
Healthcare providers 41, 62, 68, 77, 82
High levels 30, 69, 71
Hospitals 36, 68, 69, 77, 82
Human resources 15, 57, 76, 77

I

Initial Public Offerings (IPOS) 44, 45
Innovation 7, 8, 18, 19, 25, 26, 29, 38, 39, 43, 53, 66, 70, 80, 82
Innovation ecosystems 1, 29, 36, 38, 46, 51, 52, 59, 68, 69, 89
Innovation management 31, 35, 52, 53, 61, 87, 89
Innovation processes 53, 65, 80, 88
Institutions 38, 54, 60, 90
Integration 43, 44, 46, 51, 61, 62, 63, 64, 67, 68, 73, 77, 78
Intellectual property (IP) 7, 29, 53, 80, 81
Intellectual property management 52, 80, 89
Interactions 31, 33, 34, 74
Investments 12, 19, 21, 24, 26, 28, 43, 46, 53, 56, 57, 61
Investors 27, 46, 73, 80, 81, 82, 86, 89
Inter-organizational relationships (IORS) 30, 31, 32, 33, 34, 35, 36, 37, 38, 51, 52, 53, 54, 56
Italy 3, 13, 15, 16, 47, 52, 59

K

Knowledge 1, 2, 3, 36, 37, 38, 39, 40, 43, 44, 46, 47, 49, 50, 51
Knowledge-intensive industries 1, 53, 69, 80, 89

L

Laboratories 37, 41, 70, 71, 79, 88
Levels 2, 5, 8, 10, 13, 33, 60, 77
Licensing agreements 61, 64, 80, 81, 86

M

M&A (Mergers and acquisitions) 29, 30, 43, 44, 45, 46, 47, 48, 49, 50, 51
Management 12, 37, 51, 63, 71, 73, 74, 75, 78, 81
Marketing 41, 71, 72, 75, 80, 81, 82, 83, 86
Markets 19, 23, 42, 47, 48, 49, 75, 84, 90
Materials 74, 77, 84
Mechanisms 8, 49, 50, 53, 56, 70, 76, 88
Medicines 4, 19, 21, 22

Models 28, 50, 58, 59, 60, 61, 62, 63, 68, 69, 76, 85, 87

N

Networks 1, 20, 29, 36, 37, 54, 55, 56, 69
Number 10, 13, 15, 16, 18, 21, 23, 24, 40, 60

O

Objectives 6, 19, 29, 30, 31, 32, 33
Organizational capabilities 63, 65, 69, 70, 77, 78, 79, 89
Organizations 6, 29, 38, 42, 64, 67, 78

P

Partners 32, 33, 34, 35, 41, 42, 74, 82
Partnerships 24, 27, 29, 33, 39, 40, 42, 43, 51, 56, 58, 59, 60
Patents 42, 45, 55
Perspective 5, 7, 30, 31, 35, 46, 50, 53, 61, 76, 81, 87
Pharmaceutical firms 2, 9, 15, 25, 26, 36, 40, 43, 44, 45, 56, 57, 59, 60, 68
Pharmaceutical sectors 7, 11, 17, 41, 45, 82
Phases 21, 34, 44, 62, 78, 82, 88
Platforms 25, 38, 48, 49, 50, 55, 63, 67, 68, 73, 77
Players 8, 27, 34, 35
Portfolio 31, 46, 48, 57, 61
Processes 2, 4, 5, 7, 8, 28, 29, 30, 41, 42, 44, 51, 53, 62, 63, 72, 73, 74, 85
Products 18, 19, 20, 21, 22, 23, 27, 28, 39, 41, 42, 45, 53, 54, 75
Professionals 57, 65, 66, 67, 68

R

R&D (Research and development) 1, 2, 7, 8, 9, 10, 11, 15, 16, 24, 25, 26, 38, 55, 56, 57, 58, 61, 63
Regulators 25, 82, 89
Relationships 21, 35, 38, 46, 54, 73, 76, 81, 89
Research institutions 36, 53, 57, 62, 68, 80, 81, 82
Research infrastructures 38, 56, 61, 63, 71, 90
Research processes 62, 65, 66, 89
Resources 21, 37, 38, 39, 40, 42, 43, 44, 45, 54, 65, 70, 71, 76, 77, 78, 79
Revenue streams 40, 48, 55, 56, 57, 61
Risks 30, 31, 39, 40, 42, 43, 44, 46, 51, 52, 54, 61, 71, 76, 82, 83, 88

S

Safety 19, 21, 25, 82, 85
Scientific discoveries 52, 53, 55, 58, 59, 63, 64, 67, 69, 70, 71, 88, 89
Scientific innovation 76, 80, 86, 90
SDGs (Sustainable Development Goals) 80, 81, 84, 86, 87
Sector 5, 6, 8, 9, 12, 13, 16, 18, 19, 20, 21, 22, 23, 24, 26, 27, 28, 29, 30, 31, 38, 40, 41, 42, 52, 54, 70, 80, 86, 88
Service delivery 56, 58, 73, 74
Services 2, 3, 4, 8, 9, 19, 20, 25, 27, 28, 39, 42, 53, 54, 55, 58, 60, 75, 78
Skills 7, 8, 21, 32, 34, 36, 37, 39, 49, 54
South Korea 15, 52, 59, 61, 62
Spain 23, 24, 52, 59, 60
Stakeholders 23, 70, 72, 81, 82, 84, 85
Standards 12, 19, 21, 23, 32, 65, 66
Strategic architecture 63, 64, 69, 88
Strategic Management 10, 60, 65, 78
Strategic objectives 18, 31, 32, 34, 35, 36, 72, 79
Structure 5, 25, 30, 31, 32, 34, 35, 44, 46, 52, 55, 56, 57, 58, 61, 66, 67, 69, 77, 86, 88
Subsectors 1, 3, 4, 16, 17, 18, 19, 20, 21, 24, 25, 53, 81
Success 18, 35, 36, 58, 79
Supply chains 21, 31, 32, 58, 59, 75, 85
Support activities 70, 71, 72, 76, 78
Sustainability 2, 33, 37, 72, 74, 75, 81, 82, 85, 86, 87

T

Technological 53, 56, 57, 63, 64, 68, 69, 70, 71, 73, 79, 88
  Infrastructures 63, 64, 68, 71, 79, 88
  Platforms 53, 56, 57, 63, 69, 70, 71, 73, 79, 88
Technologies 3, 6, 16, 18, 27, 40, 42, 43, 44, 45, 46, 47, 48, 49, 55, 57, 58, 60, 62, 68, 77, 79, 81, 82, 88

Technology transfer 8, 59, 73, 80, 81, 82, 86, 90
Terms 10, 12, 18, 21, 31, 41, 44, 46, 47, 54, 57, 58, 75
Trajectories, strategic 40, 49, 52, 63, 88
Transformations 1, 18, 63, 64, 65, 66, 80, 88, 89, 90
Transforming 52, 53, 55, 62, 63, 66, 69, 74, 78, 85, 86, 88, 89

U

Uncertainty 40, 43, 52, 53, 56, 58, 61, 69, 71, 88
Universities 33, 40, 41, 46, 53, 56, 59, 69, 77, 85, 88, 89

V

Validation 63, 82, 83, 88
Value 24, 28, 29, 42, 43, 44, 50, 53, 54, 55, 63, 64, 70, 71, 75, 76, 77, 78, 80, 81, 87, 88
Value chain 37, 41, 43, 51, 58, 70, 71, 72, 76, 78, 84, 85, 88
Value creation 2, 28, 29, 38, 39, 43, 51, 63, 71, 80, 81, 83, 85, 86, 87
Value proposition 54, 55, 57, 82
Value system 55, 56
Ventures 46, 47, 60
Virtuous cycles 28, 33, 51, 75, 85, 87

www.ingramcontent.com/pod-product-compliance
Lightning Source LLC
LaVergne TN
LVHW070953210926
848482LV00002B/207